THE CORPORATE DIRECTOR'S FINANCIAL HANDBOOK

THE CORPORATE
DIRECTOR'S FINANCIAL
HANDBOOK

JOHN P. FERTAKIS

Q

Quorum Books

NEW YORK • WESTPORT, CONNECTICUT • LONDON

Library of Congress Cataloging-in-Publication Data

Fertakis, John P.
 The corporate director's financial handbook / John P. Fertakis.
  p. cm.
 Includes index.
 ISBN 0-89930-289-0 (lib. bdg. : alk. paper)
 1. Corporations—Finance. I. Title.
HG4026.F475 1988
658.1′5—dc 19   88-11318

British Library Cataloguing in Publication Data is available.

Library of Congress Catalog Card Number: 88-11318
ISBN: 0-89930-289-0

First published in 1988 by Quorum Books

Greenwood Press, Inc.
88 Post Road West, Westport, Connecticut 06881

Printed in the United States of America

The paper used in this book complies with the
Permanent Paper Standard issued by the National
Information Standards Organization (Z39.48-1984).

10 9 8 7 6 5 4 3 2 1

Copyright Acknowledgments

CONTENTS

FIGURES

PREFACE

The vitality of the free enterprise system and of democracy itself depends on the willing participation of people in the institutions of business and government. Citizen groups and boards are the foundation upon which actions are based and accountability is extracted. Decisions achieve their legitimacy because authority resides in duly constituted bodies composed of people of talent who have achieved prominence or who have earned the public trust.

Recent events have made it unattractive for many to serve on boards of directors, commissions, and elected bodies. This tends to deprive our institutions of the services of many people whose talents and abilities are needed to maintain the strength of the free enterprise and democratic systems of our nation. The September 8, 1986, issue of *Business Week* magazine featured this problem as its cover story, under the title "A Job Nobody Wants."

Those who serve the public in professional and elective positions have been increasingly subject to litigation, which imposes considerable financial risks as well as the potential ruin of personal reputations. Litigation issues have ranged from allegedly poor business operating decisions to the area of broad environmental issues. In its review, oversight, and control responsibilities, the board of directors is legally the highest responsible group in a business corporation. Thus the director finds himself or herself the subject of lawsuits for the failure to exercise due care in overseeing the goals of the organization and the actions of those who carry out activities.

The principle has been well established that those who take orders from superiors are not excused thereby from bearing the consequences of illegal or unethical actions. Similarly, those who guide the organization cannot take refuge in the lack of knowledge of illegal or unethical activities on the part of subordinates. Responsibility rests with the leader as well as the led. However, it is the leader who bears the brunt of ultimate responsibility.

Two approaches have developed in response to the risk of litigation and criminal or financial penalties faced by officers and board members in business organizations: insurance and competence. Insurance has been the dominant approach but has become prohibitively expensive in many cases. In addition, the extent of coverage is sometimes limited, leaving much of the risk to the individual and the organization. In some instances, insurance just cannot be obtained. Attention must then turn to improved performance and better decisions through increased competence on the part of the individual.

Courts are cognizant of the essential role played by boards, commissions, and officials and the injustice of imposing an unreasonable level of responsibility for the consequences of decisions made in good faith. But good faith must go beyond the ceremonial aspects of being in a position of high responsibility. Judgment is also an important factor. An information and experience element must enter into judgment. One should expect that a director has some knowledge of the affairs in which he or she is participating, and that some attempt is made to receive and consider information relevant to the situation or decision at hand. The best judgment of the director who has some knowledge of business affairs and who seeks relevant information cannot be legally faulted. First, poor decisions will be less likely, and second, when some decisions inevitably prove to be wrong in hindsight, placing blame may be unjustified.

It is the author's hope that this book can provide: (1) a guide to the appropriate knowledge of business operations and especially financial affairs that the director needs, and (2) an understanding of financial and related sources of information that can aid in making decisions. This book should be regarded as an introduction to the world of the corporate director. It is a book about information and relationships that can lead to a more effective role in the review, oversight, and control of corporate affairs.

THE CORPORATE
DIRECTOR'S FINANCIAL
HANDBOOK

CHAPTER 1

THE DIRECTOR'S ROLE AND FUNCTION

"We need a person of your abilities on the board of directors," says a friend, who has just treated you to lunch at the club. "John Smith has just retired and you are the logical choice to take his place." Of course you are flattered. Your friends will be impressed. This is a peak in your career. Your abilities are now about to be recognized. After discussing the opportunity with your spouse and friends, after a suitable period of introspection, and after some negotiations perhaps, you agree to have your name placed in nomination. The election takes place at the next annual meeting of the board and you are notified that you are now a member of the board of directors of the organization.

Welcome to the ranks of the corporate director. Your own route may vary somewhat from the scene above, but the important thing is that you have become a Very Important Person to a lot of people: the management, the employees and staff of the organization, the stockholders who own the corporation, the lawyers, the bankers, the U.S. Securities and Exchange Commission, the Federal Trade Commission (if the corporation does business across state lines), the citizens of the community (if the organization is a school board or other not-for-profit group), the... Wait a minute. The state? The lawyers? Bankers? The SEC? And more?

You *are* in exclusive company, and you may not have realized the full extent of your new duties and responsibilities. The consequences of your decision will gradually dawn on you. The responsibilities and obligations of being a corporate director have made the job hard to fill in many organizations.[1] But don't panic. Being a corporate director is important. Our free enterprise system operates better because people like you are there. Your knowledge is not complete, your decisions may not be 100 percent correct, outcomes will sometimes be unfavorable, so what's new?

Your legal function as a director is defined by state law, since only states can charter (create) a corporation. But most of the laws are vague. In general, a board member is elected by the stockholders and represents their rights and interests in the affairs of the corporation. Boards do not exist to run the company on a day-to-day basis. They do not have the time or expertise, and management by committees is awkward, slow, and inefficient. Thus the board appoints an executive officer, usually referred to as the president or the chief executive officer (CEO). This gives rise to a dominant theme or function of the board of directors: control and oversight of those whose function is to conduct the everyday affairs of the enterprise on behalf of the stockholders.

CONTROL

Having selected the CEO and given approval to other management selections, the board is to develop goals and policies that safeguard and enhance the interests of stockholders. The board evaluates management's performance in carrying out goals, adhering to policies, complying with laws, and maintaining its competency and integrity.

The board of directors usually forms committees in order to focus control efforts. Some committees often found are: an executive committee, a finance committee, a nominating committee, an audit committee, a public affairs committee, and a budget committee. Others can be added to the list depending on the organization and the nature of its activities. Some committees are standing committees. That is, they are continuing or permanent. Others are ad hoc, or existing only during the period of time they are necessary to deal with a specific situation. Some committees, such as an audit committee, are required by regulatory agencies, state laws, and/or by stock exchanges in which the stock is traded. In addition, special groups sometimes called "task forces" may be created to focus a variety of expertise on a difficult problem.

The function of board members on these committees is to keep abreast of various developments in the internal and/or external environment of the organization and assure that good management decisions are being made in moving toward various goals. One might think of these groups as creating a decision climate within which operating decisions can be made without a direct control function by members of the board of directors. Controls are indirect, in that appropriate goals and information brought together with well-developed alternatives can lead to appropriate decisions.

OVERSIGHT

The term *oversight* is similar in many respects to the term *control*. Both terms relate to achieving objectives through the actions of others that are in compliance with rules and desired methods of operation. Oversight refers to observing or receiving information that assures results will be as intended. It also implies an approval function that verifies important elements of operations, such as major expenditures or borrowings, and that signifies acceptance of various operating decisions and budgets.

ESTABLISHING YOURSELF AS A BOARD MEMBER

Have you wondered why you were asked to become a corporate director? Your selection may have been for a number of reasons, and they should be clear to you as you seek a useful and responsible role on the board. You may have been selected because of name recognition. A prominent golf personality is a logical choice for a golf equipment manufacturer, for example. You may have a particular area of expertise, such as public relations, law, or finance. You may have a network of connections because of your present employment—banking, advertising, or government, for instance. Perhaps you are or have been an officer of another organization important to the firm—a supplier or major customer or government regulatory agency. You may also have been selected because you can represent certain viewpoints such as minorities, environmental concerns, or the public interest. It should be obvious that another reason for your selection to the board might be that you have family connections. In any case, if you recognize the basis for your selection, it will be logical to establish yourself as best you can in that role. Be prepared to comment on those particular aspects of matters that come before the board. Raise questions in these areas if they have not been adequately considered. Offer to do homework on areas of difficulty.

It is also important that you recognize the basis of your selection and avoid possible conflicts of interest. Bringing your expertise and experience to the position is not the same as bringing proprietary or confidential information from competitors, regulatory bodies, or financial institutions. The ethical issues involved in your position on a board of directors should be recognized and possible conflicts should be avoided.

Most of your opportunities to develop your style will occur at meetings of the board and its various committees. The full board may meet monthly or perhaps quarterly. Committees may meet more frequently on an irregular basis. The size of the board varies around an average of fourteen members for Fortune 1000 companies. The number is probably fewer for smaller firms.

The board of directors often functions as a political and social body. Tact and diplomacy are important to maintaining political and social influence. Aggressiveness in challenging actions or viewpoints of others has its place, but should be reserved for those few critical matters on which you would risk your position on the board. Asking questions, providing information, identifying issues and possible consequences of actions being considered, and seeking consensus are usually more effective ways to make your point. (Chapter 8 deals with this area in more detail.)

The board often meets in a congenial environment such as a club or restaurant or an impressive board room. The agenda is usually set by the CEO or the chairman of the board, who may be one and the same person. The chairman may be a prominent or a majority stockholder, which emphasizes the need for being well informed and persuasive in a tactful manner in order to be effective. Agendas are a means for the chairman or CEO to control the board. Surprises are not welcome, and attempts to bring unscheduled matters before the board are often rebuffed. It is better to be patient and follow the due process for matters you wish to address.

The National Association of Corporate Directors (NACD) identifies four types of boards: minimum, cosmetic, oversight, and decision.[2] These represent styles of operation. Minimum boards simply meet statutory requirements and do little of importance. Cosmetic boards are a step above the minimum boards in that an attempt is made to have board members who can improve the credibility of the organization. Oversight boards more actively carry out board functions such as reviewing programs, policies, proposals, and managerial performance. They tend to consult with management more actively. Decision boards are active in setting management and organizational objectives, determining corporate policy, and authorizing various courses of action. The most prominent type of board is the oversight board, becoming a decision board in times of crisis or failure of leadership.

The U.S. Foreign Corrupt Practices Act of 1977 strengthens the oversight role in that it requires that the board assure itself that systems of control exist in the firm to prevent or disclose unlawful actions by officers and managers. As a director, it may be prudent to inquire about such controls regardless of the type of board that is in place. The act is not limited to "foreign" as the title implies. In fact, the wording of the act is taken almost directly from standards adhered to by public auditors in conducting reviews of corporate operations.

CORPORATE FINANCIAL INFORMATION:
ITS RELATION TO OPERATIONS
AND BUSINESS DECISIONS

Much of the information forming a basis for board control and oversight functions is financial information in the form of accounting reports and analyses. One may view the management and operations perspective as shown in the following diagram:

Plans are intended courses of action and uses of resources to carry out various activities. In a business organization, it is expected that activities will produce benefits for those who risk their investment in the enterprise. Activities will require the use of resources, measured in terms of costs. In not-for-profit organizations, the measurement of benefits may be on different terms than those for business organizations.

The measurement of costs and benefits in dollars reveals the extent to which management's plans and activities have met various organizational objectives. A primary organization objective is to provide a return to owners' invested capital. When benefits ("revenues" in accounting terms) are greater than costs ("expenses" in accounting terms), the profit or income represents the return to the owner's capital investment in the corporation.

Management's function is to plan activities that make the best use of the organization's resources in a profitable manner. Profitability then becomes a criterion for the board of directors' use in establishing objectives, approving plans and budgets, providing oversight, exercising control, and evaluating the organization's and the management's performance. Depending on the nature of the business, activities generally involve (1) providing a service to customers (transporting people and products for example), (2) merchandising, or buying products for resale to customers (for example, products such as home appliances, computers, etc.), (3) manufacturing products (such as toys, airplanes, etc.) or constructing (buildings, bridges, etc.).

While many businesses engage in more than one of these functions, many choose to fill only a single role. In any case, a director should understand the primary activity in which the organization is engaged and the nature of the industry in which dominant activities are carried out. Each kind of activity implies a particular control and oversight emphasis. For instance, a manufacturer must deal with questions of product design, durability and quality, and the capacity and technology of its plant and equipment. A merchandiser on the other hand must handle problems of advertising, developing a customer base, purchasing and transporting merchandise, storing and displaying goods, dealing with consumer credit, and so forth. A service organization must emphasize the quality of its people, their training, the scheduling of work, setting standards of service, and other matters. Not-for-profit organizations must carefully examine their purpose and their constituency, and carry out the various functions involved without reference to ownership considerations.

A considerable variation exists in the activities of the business enterprise, but the financial aspects lend a common focus for the director: profitability. The measurement of revenues and costs remains the common denominator in oversight, evaluation, and control.

DIRECTING THE ENTREPRENEURIAL COMPANY

Entrepreneurship has once again emerged on the business scene, if indeed it was absent. Innovation, invention, and getting started are now seen as special skills that can be learned and not solely as stemming from inborn personal characteristics. Free enterprise courses and curricula are being developed in many schools. There is no question about the need for special skills for the person who is entrepreneurial; but what of the corporate director in an entrepreneurial company?

Most of this book, and traditional management practice, is oriented to the established business enterprise. That is, a firm with (1) relatively stable product lines operating in established markets, (2) survival not being considered a primary problem, (3) key employees in place and working under well established policies, (4) an orderly turnover of people, (5) ongoing financing and investing activities, (6) reliable controls, and (7) possible *intra*preneurial activities and product champions within subunits of the organization.

The entrepreneurial company is generally somewhat new and its leadership tends to be in the hands of a younger, less-experienced management group. Management people are also more likely to be the "hands on" type of people with specialized technical abilities. The firm is quite likely to be breaking new ground in technical, economic, legal, and organizational areas. It is fast moving, probably in constant need of money, likely to have interpersonal conflicts among leaders, and is trying to develop its organizational structure and management style.

An important aspect of becoming a director in such an organization is risk. Poor decisions and bad investments are more likely than in the established organization because it is hard to resist a determined entrepreneur. Controls in such organizations are seen as restrictive and are therefore weak and difficult to implement fully. The board itself will probably be a smaller, more active, working board that meets more frequently than one in an established organization. There are probably more inside directors, and business matters for the board may seem to call for more direct and operational involvement than the indirect, review and oversight relationship.

All of this means a greater exposure to the risk of a failure to keep the stockholders' interests in mind and to remain independent of management. Bear in mind, too, that the selection of directors in entrepreneurial organizations gives emphasis to those with technical and management expertise that can be of benefit in decision making and in developing contacts and information sources in the right places.

On a more positive note, the director will find a great deal of satisfaction in such organizations. The excitement of involvement with entrepreneurial people and new business dimensions should be welcomed. The chance to reach high levels of accomplishment that require the director to bring his or her full abilities into action can be rewarding indeed.

AN ADDED NOTE ON NOT-FOR-PROFIT ORGANIZATIONS

The director of an organization that does not hold the return to ownership investment as a prominent objective will have a modified view of financial reporting, control, and oversight. These organizations include governmental bodies such as police departments, states, and municipalities; civic organizations such as libraries and public hospitals; public service organizations such as school boards, youth organizations, and chambers of commerce; and others such as private clubs, schools, churches, and labor unions.

Two primary differences exist in not-for-profit (NFP) and for-profit organizations in the cost and benefit dimensions. The accounting method employed is designed as a primary control over dollar accountability through various funds. This restricts spending to various appropriations and budget categories such as building maintenance, operations, enterprises, debt service, and others. A second primary difference is that in setting objectives and formulating plans, many costs and benefits that must be considered will not be reflected in the dollar measures portrayed in general-purpose financial reports. In planning police expenditures, for example, one benefit considered may be the decrease in dollar losses from burglaries—a social benefit that will not enter the books as revenue. An unrecorded cost might include the loss of benefits from not spending the money for street improvements or some other much-needed projects.

Directors of NFP organizations find it more difficult to balance the many demands on such organizations with the few resources usually available and to keep the appropriate beneficiaries in mind. In addition, the people receiving the benefits of expenditures may not be the same people who provide the funds, leading to many social and political dimensions in making decisions and justifying them.

CONCLUSION

Perhaps the most appropriate summary statement on the role of corporate directors is contained in a speech given by Irving S. Shapiro, chairman of E.I. duPont deNemours & Company. The board should have five basic jobs and leave the rest to their management people:

1. The determination of broad policies and the general direction the efforts of the enterprise should take.
2. The establishment of performance standards—ethical as well as commercial—against which the management will be judged, and the communication of these standards to the management in unambiguous terms.
3. The selection of company officers, and attention to the question of succession.
4. The review of top management's performance in following the overall strategy and meeting the board's standards as well as legal requirements.

5. The communication of the organization's goals and standards to those who have a significant stake in its activities (insiders and outsiders both) and of the steps being taken to keep the organization responsive to the needs of those people.[3]

Another source, a survey of board chairmen reported in 1984, indicated that among the top concerns of boards of directors in the United States are: strategic planning, top management performance and compensation, succession planning, productivity improvement, and monitoring corporate integrity.[4]

Again, welcome to the elite list of those who preside over the U.S. business scene. The responsibilities are many, but the satisfactions are there as well. The director who recognizes his or her abilities and brings due professional care and common sense to the position will not be found wanting. The remainder of this book is intended to familiarize the new director, or one who wants to know more about using information at high levels of the organization, with a quick background on a variety of topics pertinent to corporate directorship.

NOTES

1. "The Job Nobody Wants," *Business Week*, September 8, 1986, pp. 56–61; also, George Melloan, "A Good Director is Getting Harder to Find," *The Wall Street Journal*, February 9, 1988; and Myles L. Mace, Ed., "From the Boardroom," *Harvard Business Review*, July-August 1978, p. 30. See also a survey reported in a 1987 Peat Marwick & Co. brochure, *D&O—Directors' and Officers' Liability: A Crisis in the Making*. Finally, an Associated Press article by Daniel J. Wakin, "Lawsuits Cause Dearth of Corporate Directors," *The Spokesman-Review Spokane Chronicle*, May 31, 1987, p. C3, cites the results of several surveys on this problem.

2. *Evolution in the Boardroom*, National Association of Corporate Directors, Corporate Director's Special Report Series, Vol. 1, August 1978, p. 5.

3. "Corporate Governance," *The Week in Review*, Deloitte Haskins & Sells, 79–45, November 9, 1979, p. 1.

4. From a survey of board chairmen of Fortune 1000 companies by the executive search consulting firm, Heidrich & Struggles, reported in *The Week in Review*, Deloitte Haskins & Sells, 84–12, 1984.

CHAPTER 2

FINANCIAL ACCOUNTING AND REPORTING CONCEPTS

The world of the corporate director is dominated by information. Reports of all kinds must be read and digested before, during, and after meetings. Important decisions on what to do, how to do it, and how to evaluate it will be based on reports and documents of all types. Large amounts of money will be spent without ever seeing real buildings, equipment, or property in many cases.

One might think of corporate information on two levels. At one level is operating information, consisting of reports on products, sales, production, buildings and equipment, personnel, forecasts of expected developments, and other statistical information. At another level is financial information, which reflects the operating statistics in terms of dollar measures. Financial information lends a common perspective to a wide variety of organization activities. Sales of products and services provide new resources in money terms to recover production and other costs of resources used and to provide a return to stockholders for the funds they have invested. An accounting for various assets used by the business, the obligations to creditors, and the contributions of owners provide a perspective on data about revenues and costs. The accounting system is unbiased for the most part and its steady periodic or cyclical basis of reporting lends a consistency and formality to information that permits a useful assessment of the status and results of business activity.

A director should feel comfortable about the use of financial information in carrying out his or her role. The objectives of this book are to cover quickly some basics of financial information and then to explore various aspects of using such information in a higher-level organizational setting. The point of departure must be an understanding of financial reports and accounting concepts.

FINANCIAL ACCOUNTING REPORTS

Financial accounting is the term used for accounting reports that are intended for general use by outside parties such as stockholders, securities analysts, regulators, lenders, tax authorities, and others. The term *managerial accounting* refers to concepts of reporting to those who must use accounting information in decision making within the organization. For the present, the focus is on financial accounting and reporting.

There are four prominent general-purpose financial statements that are prepared for all business corporations:

1. The Statement of Income (or income statement)
2. The Statement of Financial Position (balance sheet)
3. The Statement of Changes in Financial Position (funds statement)
4. The Statement of Stockholder Equity

Supplemental reports may be added to provide details on a variety of related topics. When these titles are preceded by the term *consolidated* (Consolidated Statement of Income, for example), the report has combined the data from other organizations (subsidiaries) in which the reporting firm (parent) has an important ownership interest. Usually the criterion for consolidation is a 50 percent or greater ownership interest.

In reviewing financial statements, the director should be aware of the reporting entity or entities included. An accounting entity is any economic unit for which a complete set of accounts is maintained. For example, Wulfsberg Electronics, Inc. is owned by Sundstrand Corporation, and its financial reports are a part of the consolidated statements issued by Sundstrand Corporation. That is, Wulfsberg's assets, liabilities, revenues, and expenses are combined with those of Sundstrand for public reporting purposes.

A great deal of information is disclosed in financial statements. The apparent complexity can be overwhelming, but when reduced to its basic components, each of the four statements can be better understood. Financial statements contain various classifications of data and once the nature of a primary classification is understood one can progress to the subclassifications that provide details.

Four financial statements for Sundstrand Corporation for 1986 as found in the company's 1986 Annual Report are reproduced in the Appendix to this book. These statements—Consolidated Statement of Earnings, Consolidated Balance Sheet, Consolidated Statement of Changes in Financial Position, and Consolidated Statement of Stockholders' Equity—are part of the "financial review" section consisting of 18 pages. The other 14 pages present supplemental information on a wide variety of topics including accounting policies (always the first footnote in such reports) and other footnotes providing further information on various statement items. Also presented are financial aspects of business segments, such as product lines, overseas sales, and geographic areas. This full financial review section of Sundstrand's 1986 Annual Report is an example of the extent of financial reporting available to the public. The four statements we are discussing here can be reduced to more manageable proportions if only the main summary classifications are examined.

THE STATEMENT OF INCOME

The Statement of Income, sometimes called the Income Statement or Statement of Earnings, presents the results of operations and other events that affect the equity position of shareholders during a reporting period. Generally accepted standards of financial reporting support a classification or grouping of income statement items to make them more useful for purposes of analysis and to enhance their familiarity for readers. Income figures may be provided for: (1) income from continuing operations, before and after income taxes; (2) income after allowing for the effects of "discontinued" operations; (3) income after the effect of "extraordinary" items, such as significant gains and losses of various types; and (4) net income after noting the effects of any changes in accounting principles since the previous financial reports were issued.

Since the Sundstrand statements are relatively free of some classifications often reported by large corporations, it is instructive to look instead at the classifications required by generally accepted accounting principles. Figure 2-1 illustrates the primary classifications discussed above. Note that Sundstrand does not report any discontinued operations, extraordinary items, or changes in accounting principles during the period in its 1986 statements in the Appendix.

The director should have experienced a firsthand knowledge of all items reported below "Operating Income After Taxes." These represent major changes that should have been reviewed and approved by the full board of directors. The elements above the "Operating Income" total are not likely to have required director involvement except on a review and oversight basis.

Management should be held directly accountable for "Earnings from Operations Before Income Taxes," and should be able to explain or justify subsequent items in the report. The presence of more than a single *earnings per share* figure for a given reporting period suggests a complex stock ownership situation or significant nonoperating elements in the determination of net income.

Figure 2-1
Primary Elements of the Statement of Income
Under Generally Accepted Accounting Principles

NAME OF FIRM
Statement of Income
Date and Period of Time Reported

Revenue from the sale of goods and services

Deduct costs and expenses associated with goods sold

Equals gross profit remaining to cover indirect costs

Deduct/Add other revenues and expenses relating to operations

Equals operating income from continuing operations before taxes

Deduct provision for income taxes

*Equals operating income after provision for taxes

Discontinued operations (net of tax effect)
   Income or loss from operations discontinued during period
   Gain or loss on disposing of the discontinued segment

*Equals income before extraordinary items

*Extraordinary items gain or loss (net of tax effect)

Cumulative effect of change of accounting principles (net of tax)

*Equals net income carried into stockholders' equity

Earnings per share: reports effect of significant items in terms
   of the effect on each share of common stock, generally for
   items preceded by an asterisk (*) above.

THE STATEMENT OF FINANCIAL POSITION

The Consolidated Statement of Financial Position presents information about the cost of resources owned or controlled by the business at the date of the report. There are only three primary sections of this report: Assets, Liabilities, and Stockholders' Equity. The Asset section reports the cost of resources that are present on the balance sheet date and are presumed to have some value in future business activities. Liabilities are the amounts owed to creditors that must be repaid at specific times. Stockholders' Equity, sometimes called the Capital section, reports the amounts invested in the organization by the owners. The total cost of all assets must be equal to the sum of amounts borrowed from creditors and amounts invested by owners, hence the term *balance sheet*.

The Statement of Financial Position for Sundstrand Corporation is shown in the Appendix. Again, this report is greatly summarized from actual account

Figure 2-2
Primary Elements of the Statement of Financial Position
Under Generally Accepted Accounting Principles

```
                        NAME OF COMPANY
                  Statement of Financial Position
                        Date of Statement
```

Assets

Current Assets: Mostly cash, receivables, and inventories
   required for operations

Investments: Securities and other properties held for income or
   control

Plant and Equipment: Buildings and equipment and land

Intangible Assets: Patents, copyrights, trademarks, purchased
   goodwill, and other rights and claims

Total Assets: Those "costs" that have some potential for future
   benefits for the organization

Liabilities and Owners' Equity

Liabilities

Current Liabilities: Amounts payable to suppliers, employees,
   banks, taxes, and other creditors

Long-Term Liabilities: Long-term borrowing evidenced by notes,
   bonds, mortgages, and other indebtedness due beyond one year

Stockholders' Equity (or Capital)

Contributed Capital: Amounts received by purchasers of the
   company's ownership shares

Earned Capital: Earnings retained in the business

Total Liabilities and Owners' Equity: Sources of capitalization
   for the corporation

balances, but nevertheless presents some complex materials. The basic format for such statements as reflected in generally accepted accounting principles is shown in Figure 2-2.

For purposes of analysis, the three parts of the Statement of Financial Position are broken down into subclassifications, and then into the major categories of each classification. Assets, for example, are classified as Current Assets (consisting of cash, receivables, inventories, and so forth) and Noncurrent

Assets (such as property, plant and equipment), Intangible Assets (copyrights, patents, etc.), and Investments of a long-term nature.

Similarly, Liabilities are reported as Current Liabilities (amounts owed to vendors, banks, employees, taxes, etc.) and as Long-Term Liabilities (mortgages, notes, corporate bonds, and others). Noncurrent Assets and Long-Term Liabilities are not expected to change within the next reporting period, though transactions may occur as assets are replaced or new debt is contracted.

The Stockholders' Equity section is divided into Contributed Capital and Earned Capital in compliance with the incorporation laws of most states. Contributed Capital is the total invested by owners and evidenced by shares of stock. If the shares are assigned a dollar value (par, or stated value), amounts received in excess of that amount are shown as "additional" contributed capital (sometimes called "contributed capital in excess of par or stated value"). The practical aspects of par, no par, or stated value accounting for contributed capital are obscure and the director need not be concerned. Earned Capital, usually called Retained Earnings, is the sum of all previous earned income not having been distributed to stockholders as dividends as of the balance sheet date.

Other items are shown in the equity section of the Sundstrand balance sheet and are indicative of a variety of conditions with respect to the equity interests of stockholders. Many are beyond the scope of a book of this type. In this case, we find a foreign currency translation adjustment that represents the effects of the changing value of the U.S. dollar in comparison with the "functional" (local) currency unit used by divisions of Sundstrand that operate in other countries. (A decrease in share value from this cause is indicated in the Sundstrand report.) Chapter 12 discusses foreign operations in more depth. Another item in Sundstrand's balance sheet is Treasury Common Stock, which represents Sundstrand shares that have been repurchased by the company for some purpose but not yet used or retired. These shares remain listed above as "issued" and are subtracted in another section rather than reducing the Common Stock balance.

THE INCOME STATEMENT/ BALANCE SHEET RELATIONSHIP

The Statement of Earnings and the Statement of Financial Position are closely intertwined. In a sense, they portray a flow of costs within the business that summarizes many complexities of business activity. Figure 2-3 illustrates this cost flow.

A cost is a financial sacrifice incurred in a transaction. Thus the purchase of merchandise for resale, the purchase of a machine for use in the business, and the payment of salaries to employees involve the payment of cash or the assumption of a debt requiring future payments of cash. Creditors and the owners directly provide the cash or its equivalent initially. Subsequently, cash is generated by sales activities to continue the cycle. Let us more closely follow costs through these statements.

Figure 2-3
Overview of Accounting Flows and Reports

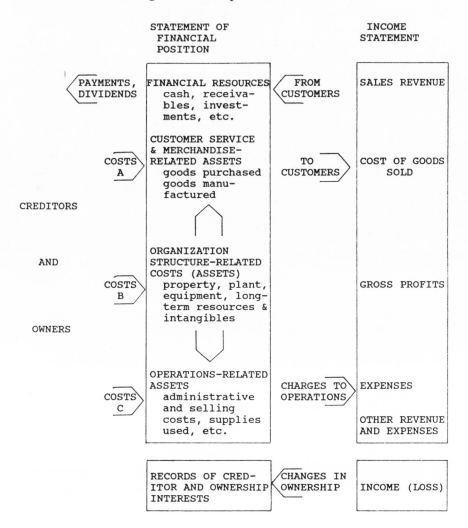

As costs are incurred, some are related to goods and services that are sold to customers to produce revenues (Costs A in Figure 2-3). These costs are then transferred to customers in exchange for new resources of cash or equivalents, and they appear on the income statement as "cost of goods sold." Unsold inventories of goods purchased or manufactured as of the balance sheet date are included among assets. Assets of this type can be seen to be costs that await future sales transactions that will produce future revenues.

The payment of salaries to employees and for business services such as advertising, insurance, and the like illustrates costs that normally flow through the balance sheet to become expenses (Costs C, Figure 2-3). At times, some of these costs have not been paid in cash at the balance sheet date or, on the other hand, cash has been paid but services have not yet been received. A residual of these transactions will appear on the balance sheet. (It can be seen that not all costs reflect cash payments in accounting procedures.)

The third type of cost (Costs B, Figure 2-3) generally determines the structure of the organization. The acquisition of land determines the place of activity. The type of machinery acquired structures the kind of manufacturing, storage, or transportation operations—and often the kinds of products to be made and sold. The acquisition of natural resources, patents, and so forth similarly structures the kinds of products and business activities that are to be undertaken. Once acquired, such costs are not generally transferred directly to customers or used up in operations. But they *do* represent costs of manufacturing, storage, display, and transportation, and thus they are allocated to customer services and merchandise-related costs and to operations over some finite period of time. This allocation is called depreciation, depletion, or amortization, and the process gradually adds these costs to the costs of goods sold or to expenses.

The income statement now shows, for the period of time being reported, the revenues earned and the various costs that were used up in the process of earning revenues. If Sales Revenues exceed the Cost of Goods Sold, and the expenses for the period, *earnings* result. The earnings are, of course, a return to owners for the risks they undertake by investing their resources in the enterprise. Note that in Figure 2-3 the creditor and ownership interests are reduced to a relatively insignificant category of "records." As creditors are paid and owners receive dividends, it is the financial resources resulting from operations that are being distributed—the assets.

Note that in this discussion the central focus is on the assets shown on the balance sheet, and accounting decisions as to the flows of these costs to the income statement to be matched against revenues in determining income. Management and stockholders, on the other hand, commonly focus on the income statement as the primary document. This is a significant point of departure in the financial role of the director.

Where is the "real" value of the firm? Is it on the balance sheet, where costs of resources invested and available for future operations are shown as of a calendar date? Or is it reflected in the ability of the firm to generate and collect revenues in excess of costs over a period time? This difference of opinion will be considered in a broader context as this book progresses. Additional light is shed on the Statement of Income and the Statement of Financial Position by the other two primary reports, the Statement of Changes in Financial Position and the Statement of Stockholders' Equity.

Figure 2-4
Statement of Changes in Financial Position
Under Generally Accepted Accounting Principles
(as of 1988 to be called the Statement of Cash Flows)

NAME OF COMPANY
Statement of Changes in Financial Position
For period of time being reported

CAPTION	EXPLANATION
Operating Activities	Explains the changes in cash or working capital due to normal operations of buying, manufacturing, and selling goods or services
Dividends Paid	Earnings distributed to shareholders
Investing Activities	Cash or working capital used or received by acquiring or disposing of noncash assets
Financing Activities	Cash or working capital paid out or received from borrowing or repaying debt or from selling or repurchasing owner shares
Change in Cash Funds	The amount by which cash and cash equivalents have increased or decreased since the first of the year

CONSOLIDATED STATEMENT OF CHANGES IN FINANCIAL POSITION

The Funds statement supplements the balance sheet and income statement by highlighting the financial effects of major areas of activity or business decisions. Its major sections are reviewed in Figure 2-4. The Financial Accounting Standards Board has changed the nature of this report significantly and those experienced in past renditions of fund statements should be aware of the new format, to be called the Statement of Cash Flows.

This statement includes a number of adjustments to income statement and balance sheet figures to extract the basic resource flows that have been somewhat obscured by the requirements of accounting income determination. For example, sales to customers is essentially a cash inflow and is reduced in accounting by costs of merchandise sold, general expenses, and allocated costs of plant assets (depreciation). The latter are not cash payments however. Hence net earnings are not representative of operating cash inflows and outflows to the extent that noncash items like depreciation expenses have been deducted from revenues. The Funds Flow statement shows that depreciation expenses have been added to net earnings to cancel or offset the noncash expenses and show the cash provided by operations relating to transactions with customers. The

Sundstrand Corporation Statement of Changes in Financial Position in the Appendix contains several adjustments of this type.

The Investing Activities section of the Statement of Changes highlights major decisions in acquiring or disposing of structure-related assets. These are transactions with a major balance sheet impact and often involve complex strategic decisions by management and the board of directors.

The section on Financing Activities sets forth major stockholder- and creditor-related transactions. The impact of these changes on the interests of various participants in the organization's financial structure is again indicative of economic and strategic objectives of the management and directors. A more complete discussion of financing and investing decisions is presented in Chapter 11.

Those who equate earnings with net cash inflows into the organization are sometimes confused by the apparent lack of relationship between earnings and cash. A firm with a succession of operating losses may in fact have a growing cash balance, or vice versa. Some firms continue in business for a surprising length of time without profits, and firms with profits may be unable to repay creditors and find themselves in bankruptcy. The Statement of Changes in Financial Position highlights the ability of operations to provide an inflow of cash and working capital, and provides details of nonoperating sources and uses of financial resources. The director should find in this statement a useful summary of what should have been significant board of directors deliberations over the reporting period.

THE STATEMENT OF STOCKHOLDERS' EQUITY

The fourth major statement summarizes activities that affect the status of the Stockholders' Equity accounts. Where such changes are few and infrequent, they may be disclosed in the footnotes section of the financial reports and a simple Statement of Retained Earnings may be reported. These data may even be included in the Stockholders' Equity section of the Balance Sheet and not in a separate statement.

The major sections of this statement depend on the way in which the corporation is capitalized and other variables. Figure 2-5 illustrates some possible items one might find.

In most cases, each stockholder equity classification will display the first-of-the-year balance, additions, subtractions, and end-of-the-period balance. Most stockholder's equity transactions are rare, with the exception of changes in the retained earnings of the corporation. The major recurring change in stockholder equity is the change in the "Retained Earnings" category. In the accounting process at the end of the reporting period, income statement accounts are closed and the results (net earnings or profit) are added to the retained earnings beginning balance. The resulting total represents the owners' reinvestment of earnings since the inception of the corporation. Finally, the amount of this total

Figure 2-5
Statement of Stockholders' Equity
Under Generally Accepted Accounting Principles

NAME OF COMPANY
Statement of Stocholders' Equity
Date of Report

CAPTION	EXPLANATION
Contributed Capital (see note below)*	Section lists amounts received from the sale of securities to owners and from other types of ownership transactions
Preferred stock, if any	Stock with a specific ownership prefer- ence, usually a dividend requirement
Common stock	Stock designated as residual and without limitation on participation in owner rights
Additional paid in capital	Amounts received above that designated as par or stated value assigned to the shares issued
Earned Capital	Past and present earnings not distri- buted to owners
Retained Earnings	Amount technically available for distri- bution to owners
Appropriated	Amount identified by board action as being unavailable for declaration as dividends
Treasury Stock	Shares of the company's own stock that have been repurchased for some purpose (shown at cost)

```
*EACH CLASSIFICATION IS USUALLY DISCLOSED AS FOLLOWS:
  Balance at beginning of period                  $ xxxx
  Additions to account balance       (detail        xxxx
  Deductions from account balance    shown)        (xxxx)
  Balance at end of period                        $ xxxx
```

that has been distributed to stockholders during the current period (dividends) is subtracted to yield the ending total.

The growth in most businesses is financed by the retention by the corporation of a portion of earnings. In only a few instances will one find that all earnings in any single period will be declared as dividends. The distributions to stock- holders are generally less than the earnings reported for the period. The direc- tors will often find compelling reasons for retaining a significant portion of earnings. As costs of goods and services used by the business rise during inflationary times or periods of scarcity, some earnings must be retained just to maintain a stable base of assets and operations.

Dividend policies in some organizations may be independent of earnings in the short run. The board of directors may establish a fixed annual dividend amount designed to enhance the company's stock as an investment. A long period of steady dividends and a growing company are highly desirable characteristics that promote a stable base of stock ownership. Some firms strive for growth through internal financing and may have only token dividends if any. The director may wish to develop some longer-range policies on dividends rather than having to decide on dividends each year.

The category called Treasury Stock shows the number and cost of the company's own stock that has been reacquired for some purpose. It also reports the distribution of treasury shares and the purpose, such as for executive stock option plans. The shares so acquired remain classified as issued and outstanding for practical purposes.

In viewing the Sundstrand Consolidated Statement of Stockholders' Equity in the Appendix, it can be seen that changes have occurred in all of the categories of stockholders' equity accounts in the three-year period being reported. It is beyond the scope of this book to explain the technical aspects of pensions, acquisitions, stock option plans, and restricted stock issues referred to in some of the account changes. The corporate director will find many kinds of complex transactions reflected in financial reports and should not hesitate to ask for a complete explanation by appropriate officers such as the treasurer or controller. Some explanation is found in the Notes to Financial Statements part of financial reports (Notes for the Sundstrand Corporation are shown in the Appendix.) The director should be aware that the footnotes are an integral part of the financial statements and are intended to provide additional information about complex situations. They are not intended to *simplify* reported data.

CONCLUSION

This chapter has presented the four primary financial statements issued by business corporations: the Statement of Earnings, the Statement of Financial Position, the Statement of Changes in Financial Position, and the Statement of Stockholders' Equity. More commonly used terms for discussing these statements are: the Income Statement, the Balance Sheet, the Funds Statement, and the Statement of Capital (or, simply, the Statement of Retained Earnings).

Financial statements are the most common kinds of reports received by the board of directors. The income statement and the balance sheet should be provided quarterly at a minimum. Securities markets, various levels of taxing authority, bankers, credit rating agencies, and others usually mandate quarterly financial reports (interim reports), and these should be viewed and approved for issuance by the board. The quarterly financial reports present the opportunity for control and oversight as well. When accompanied by comparable data for the previous quarter, the same quarter for the previous year, or by budgeted expectations, a meaningful basis for comparison is evident.

An active board may want reports on a monthly schedule, but this practice may not be the best in terms of oversight and control. The time period is too short to allow a good evaluation of performance toward corporate goals. In addition, frequent operating reports have the effect of drawing the directors into an involvement with day-to-day operating decisions and problems, diverting attention from a longer-term perspective. If the need for a closer monitoring of management actions is evident, an executive committee could be formed for that purpose. More detailed financial reporting on a more frequent basis would be appropriate for such a committee. These reports should be managerial accounting reports, which are elaborated upon in Chapter 5.

CHAPTER 3
INTERPRETING FINANCIAL INFORMATION

It has been demonstrated in Chapter 2 that financial statements present to the viewer a great deal of information. The statements are often lengthy, even though the data they present have been greatly aggregated and summarized from the underlying accounting system. Further summarizations are usually made by users of financial reports, depending on the individual's focus and tolerance for details.

The director's focus on oversight and control can be approached for now by looking at only a few interpretive measures of business performance. Any measure of performance is going to motivate management behavior in a manner consistent with the measurement. The director should be cautious in setting goals, choosing the measurement, and evaluating results. More on this as the book progresses.

Corporate performance is brought about by people, products, and services, and by the skillful management of these factors and their costs. Financial reports and financial analysis merely track that performance and draw attention to evaluation and decision-making factors. Good performance, by any criteria one chooses, should also result in good financial results. While performance is not the same as its measurement in financial terms, one finds that they are closely linked in the management process of motivating, evaluating, or rewarding people.

Five common financial performance measures that should be understood and evaluated by directors are discussed in this chapter. A more extensive compilation of various financial analysis tools is beyond the scope of this book and beyond the basic needs of the director. The computation of financial ratios has not been standardized. The variety of methods for computing these ratios can make comparisons difficult. Hence, caution is advisable in making *inter*firm comparisons. But certainly *intra*firm compilations of various years' or several departments' ratios should be assumed to be consistent and therefore useful for comparisons.

RETURN ON INVESTMENT

The highest level of aggregation in financial analysis is the return on investment (ROI). This measure reduces the income statement and the balance sheet to a ratio of the most significant and summary figures in each statement. These are the net earnings and the investment, computed as:

$$\frac{\text{net earnings}}{\text{average investment}} = \text{return on investment}$$

The term *investment* may be computed in different ways. It may mean: (1) common stockholders' equity, (2) total stockholders' equity, (3) stockholders' equity plus long-term debt, (4) total assets, or some other combination. In the computation of (3) and (4), income taxes and interest on long-term debt are added back to net earnings. This represents the view that taxes and interest are distributions of earnings to the larger equity group being included and therefore have been "earned" on the larger investment base represented.

The director's focus is usually the return to total stockholders' equity (2), and that is the emphasis reflected here. In many decisions, someone will ask, "What is the 'bottom line'"? By this is meant the net earnings or the effect of the decision at hand on the net earnings or on the ROI calculation. This may not be the best point to emphasize for every situation, but it is commonly done in order to simplify a complex set of data.

The ROI concept is relatively recent. It arose in the early part of the twentieth century as a control tool. It was a means by which corporations with multiple divisions and multiple products could establish measurable performance criteria for managers of diverse activities. Directors and central management groups were often unable to evaluate rationally how well sales were made and costs incurred in far-flung and complex operations. ROI was also instrumental in deciding where capital investments should be employed for the greatest benefit, and it remains so today.

To those who regard the sole purpose of business activity to be the maximizing of the financial interests of owners, the ROI tells it all, or at least most of it. It is a mistake, though, to use this measure for oversight and control. There are short-term and long-term aspects. ROI can be maximized in the short run while sacrificing the future of the firm. For example, managers may reduce or discontinue spending on research, advertising, maintenance, insurance, safety, equipment replacement, and so forth and thus raise ROI for one or more reporting periods until disaster strikes. In some cases, needed modernization and capital improvements are not made because the effect will be to increase investment and thus reduce ROI.

ROI should be considered as a useful gauge of performance, *subject to* maintaining the integrity and safety of the investment by stockholders, operating the firm in a legal manner, and maintaining the flow of products and services in such a manner as to attract and keep customers. This suggests additional summary ratios that can aid in measuring these other factors and providing the incentive for managers to watch more than one aspect of operations.

PROFITABILITY AND INVESTMENT TURNOVER

Within the oversight and control frame of reference, it is useful to analyze the methods by which management can affect the ROI measure. Two significant components constitute the total ROI and provide the second and third financial measurements of importance to the director: return on sales (profitability), and investment turnover. By examining the components, the director can discern the underlying management strategies by which ROI is affected. The relationships are expressed as follows:

$$\frac{\text{net earnings}}{\text{net sales}} \times \frac{\text{net sales}}{\text{average investment}} = \frac{\text{net earnings}}{\text{average investment}} = \text{ROI}$$

The relationship of net earnings to net sales is often the primary measurement of the efficiency of operations. In that sense, a combination of a watchful eye over costs and an astute sense of the market and pricing strategies is a hallmark of good management. The term *profitability* is associated with the return on sales.

The investment turnover ratio measures other dimensions of management performance: the ability to manage assets wisely and keep them at an appropriate level, and the ability to keep sales at a high level relative to the resources used.

ROI can be increased by raising the profitability of sales and/or by increasing sales or reducing investment. Most management control efforts are at first directed to raising profitability (sales price analysis and cost analysis and control). But a more sustaining means of ROI improvement may be to increase the sales level or to reduce investment dollars. However, this assumes that sales can be increased without raising costs and expenses that reduce net earnings. By watching both figures over a few reporting periods, the director can better understand *how* management is achieving ROI results or *why* performance is declining.

If ROI is an important goal and measure of performance, management may be encouraged to delay needed investments in research, plant and equipment replacement, or other actions with strategic (long-term) importance. A director should be alert to various games that can be played to satisfy ROI goals, and these two performance measures can be very useful.

DEBT/EQUITY RATIO

The relationship of total outstanding noncurrent debts, such as bonds and mortgages, to the stockholders' equity investment is of importance in evaluating the way in which the firm has balanced its sources of capital. The calculation of the fourth ratio is:

$$\frac{\text{total noncurrent debt}}{\text{total stockholders' equity}} = \text{debt to equity (\%)}$$

The ability of the corporation to borrow money or sell its stock may hinge on this relationship. It seems appropriate that the greatest risk should be undertaken by owners, who also stand to receive the greatest benefit if the firm is successful. A high proportion of debt, which must be serviced by paying interest whether the firm is successful or not, reduces earnings available to stockholders.

If debt borrowed at a 10 percent rate of interest is invested in assets and operations producing a 15 percent return on the investment, stockholders will benefit by the difference. This is sometimes referred to as "trading on the equity." For example, if $1 million is borrowed at 10 percent, annual interest will be $100,000. When this $1 million is invested in operations producing a 15 percent return, or $150,000 annually, the $50,000 left after covering interest expense will benefit the owner group. Incurring debt can therefore be an attractive means of financing.

In a technical sense, financial analysts use a "weighted average cost of capital" in looking at the cost of investment resources. This means that an investment is not evaluated solely on the basis of the specific cost of the money obtained, but on the mix of debt and equity financing that comprises the funds used. Ideally, the return on the investment of resources should be greater than this average if stockholders are to achieve a real benefit.

A desirable debt to equity ratio is dependent on the specific firm, industry, and the particular circumstances involved. In most firms and among most analysts, some optimum relationship of debt and equity financing exists. Management tends to maintain some amount of debt on the balance sheet. A large change in this ratio should be related to some past decision of the board of directors. If not, it should spark pointed inquiries from board members.

WORKING CAPITAL RATIO

Most of the activities of a business that produce revenues from the sale of products and services are found in accounts related to current assets, current liabilities, and sales and expenses. At a given time, balance sheet accounts that freeze this motion are found in current assets and current liabilities. This is the capital investment that is working. Working capital is the dollar amount of current assets minus total current liabilities. It is the dollar amount of noncurrent debt and equity that is involved in operating the business.

Resources to sustain current operations, pay for long-term assets, pay interest on debt, pay income taxes, and to pay dividends to stockholders must be produced by this capital that is at work. Thus there is much interest in performance as indicated by this measure. Since a dollar total for working capital is hard to interpret or evaluate, analysts prefer a ratio measurement computed as follows:

$$\frac{\text{current assets}}{\text{current liabilities}} = \text{working capital ratio}$$

Most textbooks cite a 2:1 ratio as a minimum expectation for the working capital ratio. This implies that there are twice as many dollars in current operations as are needed to pay current creditors if necessary. Another interpretation is that if operations are terminated, current assets could be sold at half their recorded values and still produce a sufficient amount to repay the current debt outstanding. While there are inaccuracies in both assumptions, such standards have been perpetuated and are used. A wide variation in average current ratios among industrial segments of the economy indicate a situational context in interpreting the current ratio.

The relationship of various accounts in the working capital "cycle" is illustrated in Figure 3-1. The items in Figure 3-1 that are enclosed in boxes are accounts that are found on the balance sheet, while the others are shown on the income statement. The two statements are thus intertwined in reporting on the operating results of the business. The amount of capital obtained from long-term creditors and owners that is involved in these central business activities is obviously an important item for the director to watch.

An additional important measure involving working capital is the operating cycle or cash conversion cycle. This computation permits an interesting comparison of the number of days that are required to recover resources expended in operations. This figure is a combination of the number of days required to collect sales made on account and the number of days required to sell the inventory. The computation is:

Figure 3-1
The Working Capital Cycle

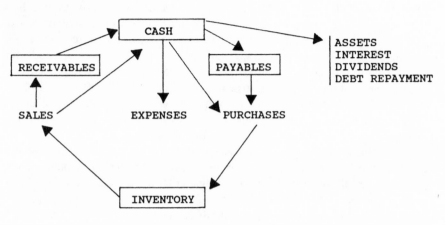

$$\frac{\text{average accounts receivable}}{\text{sales} \div 365} + \frac{\text{average inventory}}{\text{cost of goods sold} \div 365} = \text{days}$$

In other words, once inventory is purchased, how many days does it require to recover the cash spent?

The operating cycle in days can be expected to differ depending on the nature of the activity. One would expect, for example, that a furniture store would have a much longer period than a grocery store. A routine examination of current accounts can be seen to give some important insights into the operations of the business.

SINGLE AND MULTIPLE PERFORMANCE CRITERIA

Five important measures of performance criteria for evaluation have been presented. Which is most relevant for oversight and control? Should one be regarded as the target for management effort, or should management be expected to work toward goals in all five—or even more than five—areas? The answer is not easy.

Business should be operated in a balanced fashion, and financial reports should report on that balance. However, managers know they are being evaluated and tend to structure their performance to maximize those performance measures that they perceive to be the most highly regarded and rewarded by superiors. Multiple measures require trade-offs to maintain a balanced set of results. But how does the manager decide among those trade-offs? For example, if the manager offers more liberal credit terms to customers, sales can be increased, resulting in a higher ROI. But the increase in receivables is accompanied by a higher payables amount for inventory purchases and for bank credit to finance the additional inventories and receivables, thus decreasing the current ratio. Increasing losses from uncollectible accounts receivable will also reduce earnings. These effects may be reduced by some other actions with even more subtle effects. Some effects of using a single measure of performance such as ROI have already been discussed.

If multiple measurement criteria are used, it may quickly become evident that directors or managers regard some as more important than others, and performance follows accordingly. If a single criterion is used, it also becomes evident that superiors are concerned with others as well, and again performance will reflect the perceptions of the responsible person. One can imagine a fire department being awarded a certificate for success in fire prevention efforts while at the same time being cited for having the highest cost per fire in the region. Which is most important?

WHAT FINANCIAL STATEMENTS DON'T TELL YOU UNLESS YOU LOOK

The financial statements of a business will report on what happened in dimensions that can be measured in financial terms. They do not explain how or why the results are as reported, but they may suggest qualitative factors that are important. Several aspects of performance are key factors in producing the results reported. Some of these are discussed briefly here.

Product Quality

An important determinant of sales revenues and the cost of products sold is the quality factor. Costs can be reduced at the expense of quality, but decreased sales are likely to follow. Is this why sales are down this year? Higher spending for product design and reliability factors can raise product costs and reduce profits unless the sales price is higher. An increase in the sales price can reduce sales volume in units while total sales revenue in dollars can remain the same. Financial reports do not explain the underlying factors that produce the observed results. Managers should be able to provide directors with explanations based on internal managerial accounting reports and analyses.

Relations with Customers and Suppliers

Customer relationships influence sales revenue and vendor relationships can affect the cost of merchandise that is sold. Businesses spend a great deal of time and money to advertise and promote and attractively display their products and services. Once they attract customers it is surprising how little may then be done to keep them. There are maintenance costs that should be expected and willingly spent for customer loyalty. A business should deliver merchandise and services as promised, repair things if they are faulty, replace them if the customer is not satisfied, listen to and respond to complaints, provide the services the customer expects, be sure bills sent to customers are correct, and assure that customer payments are promptly recorded. These maintenance costs may seem to reduce profits in the short run, but yield increasing sales revenues and profits later.

The selection and treatment of vendors (those who supply the firm with inventory and services) has a strong effect on the cost of merchandise and services sold. If these costs are increasing or are larger than industry averages or those reported by competitors, a problem may exist. The level of costs can be influenced by the terms of sale and the discounts available, the distance over which goods must be transported to reach the buyer's facility, the carrier selected, insurance costs, the reliability of the vendor for quality products and on-time deliveries, the size of and frequency of orders, and numerous other factors.

Employee Relations

Labor costs affect both the costs of products manufactured and selling and administrative expenses. Employees stand in a delicate balance between effective operations and cost efficiency. Effectiveness is a term used to describe actions that are oriented toward the attainment of objectives, while efficiency refers to doing so at a minimum cost. The important ingredient here is good labor relations.

Wages and salaries paid to employees may be high because the firm is offering attractive wage rates and fringe benefits or, conversely, because the firm is offering low wages and inadequate benefits. In the first case, poor operating policies, a slow pace of operations, or inadequate investments in machinery, tools, and technology may keep productivity from reaching its potential even with a stable, well paid, and highly motivated work force. In the second case, the firm may be unable to attract and retain good employees. A high level of training costs, excessive absenteeism, high labor turnover rates, and poor employee morale and loyalty can negate the potential of good operating procedures and good investments in machinery, tools, and technology.

When it is determined that inadequate financial results on the income statement are due to employee relations problems, the director should expect many complex issues and no simple answers. Unlike correcting an errant machine with a quick replacement, labor relations difficulties take a long time to correct. Neither money nor technology can effect a quick fix. Directors should look at labor turnover rates, the number of grievances filed, accident rates, absenteeism, union problems and negotiations, and comparative wage rates in the community in order to develop a feel for wage and salary costs and factory labor costs that may seem out of line. The corporate controller and the managerial accounting functions should be able to accumulate and report on many of these measurements.

The Competitive Environment

The level of sales revenue that one finds on the income statement is influenced by a great many factors that can be grouped here as either market segmentation and pricing strategy, or as market share and market growth.

Market Segmentation and Pricing Strategy. Most businesses are characterized as broadly based within industry segments such as furniture manufacturing, metal products, transportation, insurance, or other industrial classifications. Appliance stores, for example, stock and sell refrigerators, dishwashers, clothes washers and dryers, vacuum cleaners, toasters, microwave ovens, irons, and a variety of other products. They also tend to price various lines of merchandise at low, medium, and high prices. Thus they attempt to serve the needs and income levels of many potential buyers of appliances. This is a traditional concept of business activity with which most consumers are familiar. Sales revenue is a combination of sales of many individual kinds of products and various pricing strategies. These prices tend to be established over years of doing business in a fixed location and by following industry trends.

An aggressive newcomer in business may find it difficult to compete "head to head" against an established firm as described above. Rather than compete at all pricing levels and product lines, a competitor may choose one line of merchandise such as vacuum cleaners and floor care products, and/or only one level of prices. The combination of product specialization and price strategy has the effect of segmenting the market. The trucking industry did this to the railroads and the airline companies did it to the truckers as transportation services became segmented. The automobile companies have long practiced segmentation of products and markets by customer income levels.

One can see that strategies that involve high pricing also tend to reduce volume, and vice versa. Both strategies can maintain or improve profits in the existing competitive environment. The Lincoln automobile dealer can operate just as profitably as the Chevrolet dealer despite wide variations in the price, volume, and cost of the product.

Despite the effectiveness of a competitor in a segmented market, many full-line businesses continue to carry product lines impacted by specialty stores because of the full-service concept. That is, even though sales and profits are low in one price range or one type of product, the manager feels it is important to be able to meet the needs of all of the store's customers and continues to carry the product. The director may want to inquire about the competitive environment, market segmentation, and the firm's strategies.

Market Share and Market Growth. Any given area of business endeavor is faced with a finite potential number of customers. In any given accounting period, one can ascertain through various sources how many sales were made in the industry. That is, the market in any given period consists of all units sold by all competitors. An important statistic in evaluating a business is its share of that total market. An important strategic factor is the extent to which the market is expected to increase or decrease. Marketers look for ways to maintain the business's share of the market and to enlarge its share if possible. If the market is growing, added sales should result as a simple matter of course. If the market is declining, it is important to develop a coherent strategy to maintain sales levels or reduce costs or to develop alternative products to revive the market or enter new markets.

These performance criteria are seldom available to the board of directors in routine reports. It may be advisable to have an occasional report from the marketing department or to have a marketing executive present at board meetings when issues relating to products and pricing are discussed.

A great deal of marketing literature tends to emphasize "product portfolios" in developing strategies relating to market share and growth. Within a given firm, there should be products at various stages of development as to share and growth characteristics. It is the total return produced by all products in the portfolio that reveals how well balanced the firm's marketing strategy is . The director may well ask which products are in high-share and low-growth markets and what is being done with the cash typically provided by such product sales.

The State of Factory Facilities and Technology

Financial statements disclose the cost and depreciation of plant facilities (buildings, equipment, tools, conveyors, vehicles, etc.), and the amounts spent for new facilities and received on the sale of old ones. The dollar figures are informative, but do not disclose the adequacy of these assets for the purposes they serve. They do not indicate their state of repair and maintenance or the technology represented in these assets.

One would expect that an organization with a large investment in plant facilities would incur a relatively constant amount of cost for replacing assets that have become worn out, obsolete, inadequate, or superseded by newer technology. A rising level of sales would suggest additional expenditures for the expansion of plant facilities. The director can watch the amounts shown on the statement of financial position for plant and equipment, and can compare with the investments and disinvestments in these assets as shown on the statement of changes in financial position.

This quick reference may lead to questions pertinent to the oversight and control function. Recall that the measurement of "return on assets" can be improved by delaying replacement expenditures. Depreciation charges for existing plant serve to reduce the book value of total assets (asset cost less the accumulated depreciation). Several accounting periods later, the earnings figure will be affected as the cost of goods sold and operating expenses begin to reflect the higher costs of keeping older plant facilities operating. About this time, problems with product quality and customer relations begin to reduce sales revenues and the firm is approaching real difficulties.

Organizations with fewer plant assets differ in that replacement and new plant expansion costs tend to be less evenly incurred. A major plant cost may follow several years of no such expenditures. The director should look at the longer-term record or ask management for advance notice of planned expenditures for plant and equipment, perhaps up to five years in the future. A more rational plan for financing can then be constructed.

Inventories

Most firms carry too much investment in inventories and supplies. The purpose served by inventories is to decouple management decisions about purchasing or manufacturing from the management of sales. It is wise and cost efficient to schedule a level rate of production despite a fluctuating or seasonal pattern of sales. This eases the responsibilities of production and marketing officers to coordinate the two functions. The investment in production facilities might also be lower because the need for capacity to respond to a period of high sales is decreased by the ability to build inventories to meet the expected demand. The cost of having inventories may be high, however. Inventories tend to build up when sales are at seasonal lows, requiring the incurrence of costs for storage space, insurance, inventory taxes, handling costs, and the indirect costs of the risk of damage, obsolescence, and theft.

One concept that has been used advantageously by the Japanese and some domestic firms is the "just-in-time" inventory control. If purchasing and manufacturing can be made more responsive to sales patterns, the inventory buildup is diminished. Several techniques exist to smooth the flows of inventories and production processes to accomplish a recoupling of purchasing, manufacturing, and sales functions. Experience has shown that the reduced space required because of the absence of inventory storage needs can offset the possible added equipment capacity costs. A major benefit as well as problem is the response of functional management people who may be required to reestablish cooperation and communication with each other. The director should not be expected to have expertise in these operating areas, but by watching inventory levels and cost of sales trends, a few well-phrased questions may move management to improve its performance.

Inventories that are not moving should be disposed of at bargain prices or discarded. Both represent losses that should be recognized in the reporting period when the loss is evident; and herein lies a major oversight problem for the director. Managers responsible for profitable operations are often reluctant to dispose of these items and have the reduction in earnings become evident. Routine inventory losses are to be expected and recognized as a part of the cost of doing business, but in a close situation it may seem harmless to avoid the write-down if possible. After all, there is still some chance the merchandise may still be sold at full price, they reason. As cumulative decisions to avoid recognizing these losses produce bloated inventory figures in the accounts and in the warehouse, the decision to write down is harder to make.

One of the functions of both internal and public auditors is to examine the inventories in both the accounts and the storage and display areas. If the potential for sales revenue is low, the auditors should strongly urge management to write down and dispose of these items. Auditors should be able to attest that they have examined the inventories and the valuation methods and physical controls used and that the figures can be relied upon.

All inventory costs on a given date should appear in the caption "inventories" on the balance sheet and in the "cost of goods sold" on the income statement. The director should be aware of changes in the amounts and relationships of these accounts as clues to potential organization problems. Inventories as a percentage of total current assets and cost of goods sold as a percentage of sales revenues should hold relatively constant most of the time.

Inventory Quality

Inventories of merchandise for resale, or materials for future production requirements, represent a particularly difficult measurement and control problem. A merchandising firm buys goods from manufacturers or wholesalers and then stores, displays, and delivers them to customers without materially adding to the product's basic characteristics. The purchasing function is carried out by a purchasing officer or agent who processes requests from sales managers and locates sources of supply of the required quality at the best price and terms of sale.

A manufacturing firm buys materials (raw materials, component parts, etc.) for fabrication into the company's products. The cost of materials used, factory labor employed, and a charge for general factory costs called overhead become the cost of goods manufactured, another inventory classification.

A service firm (bank, university, club, hotel, auto repair shop, etc.) may have incidental inventories that are used in the services provided to customers, but the primary emphasis is on labor, which cannot be stored for future use. Such inventories are called supplies and may present the same difficulties that merchandisers and manufacturers experience.

In most firms, at least some of the costs represented by inventory accounts are of doubtful value. Items that are in large quantities while sales are slow are a waste of capital. More importantly, some items may have practically no sales potential at all. Such costs should be written down, or charged to expenses, if the decline in value is deemed to be permanent. This write down may be resisted by management on several grounds. The reduction in reported income for the period may reflect unfavorably on a manager's performance. In addition, it may be argued that the auditor's judgment that the items have suffered a permanent decline in value may not be as good as the salespeople's confidence that the product will in fact prove to be salable eventually. These decisions are not easy and may cause many hard feelings.

Inventories usually account for a major portion of working capital. It thus pays to control inventories carefully. Accounting controls and physical protection systems should be designed to safeguard this investment, and it is often the auditors who examine and evaluate the systems and the information derived from them. The audit committee of the board of directors should have access to the auditors' reports and recommendations regarding all inventories.

CONCLUSIONS

Five important areas of evaluation of organizational performance were presented in this chapter. Ratios that summarize some of these areas were discussed. The latter part of the chapter presented a look at some things that financial statements and ratios might not reveal for the purposes of review, oversight, and control by the director. However, it is evident that many clues lie in the figures. Much can be found out by using the numbers as clues to what managers ought to be able to tell the board. Finally, the identification of important figures and relationships may be of some assistance in developing some single or multiple criteria by which management and organizational performance can be guided and evaluated.

CHAPTER 4

THE NATURE OF AUDITS
AND AUDIT COMMITTEES

Auditors check up on and evaluate the work done by others. This chapter is concerned with the work of *accounting* auditors and the impact of their efforts on the oversight and control function of the director.

The auditing function of the certified public accountant (CPA) is justified in the need for reliable financial information that permits the smooth functioning of the free enterprise economy. Users of financial data generally have little if any contact with the day-to-day affairs of the business. If they could not trust the financial statements to reflect business performance adequately, the institutions of banking and stock exchanges could not exist as they do today.

Auditors have a responsibility to search for material—that is, significant—conditions that may make financial reports misleading. This would certainly include fraud, errors, and employee actions contrary to management's policies, as well as failure to follow generally accepted principles of accounting and reporting.

Financial reports are the representations of the management of the business. Public auditors can only render an opinion on these reports. They cannot themselves change them or prevent management from issuing them. However, if a material misstatement is found, management can be strongly motivated to make the necessary changes lest the auditor warn of the problems in the "Opinion," which becomes a part of the financial statements. It should be noted that the Securities and Exchange Commission (SEC) will not accept a registrant's financial statements if the auditor's opinion is modified to point out a misstatement or omission that the management could rectify.

LEVELS OF AUDITING

There are several levels of financial audit in a business organization. The most obvious is the public, or external, audit. Most public business audits are performed by CPAs who are members of public accounting firms. The larger the organization and the more far-flung are its operations, the more likely it will need a large CPA firm to assure the required accounting resources, independence, and continuity offered by them. A degree of prestige is provided by having a "big eight" accounting firm as the auditors of record.[1] It is a responsibility of the board of directors to select or approve the firm that is to conduct the audit.

A second level of audit is provided by internal auditors. These are accountants who are employees of the business. The accountant who does not offer services to the general public but is employed by a business organization is known as a private accountant. A CPA certification is not required for private accountants, though some do possess the certificate. Other evidence of professional competence is provided by such recognitions as the CMA (certificate in management accounting), the CIA (certified internal auditor), and others, though a professional designation is not required. Internal auditors are customarily separate from the general accounting and bookkeeping functions that operate the ongoing system for processing accounting transaction data.

The internal auditor plays a similar role to that of the external auditor: checking up on the accounting and bookkeeping function, assuring that accounting controls and administrative controls are in place, assuring that they are effective, and assuring that financial data can be relied upon to represent the financial affairs of the organization. The board of directors should make certain that the internal audit is being performed and that auditors are independent and have the freedom to conduct inquiries and report to appropriate organizational levels. In general, the board of directors creates an audit committee to work closely with both internal and external auditors.

Other levels of audit are usually embedded in the operating systems of the organization and are sometimes referred to as internal controls, and they may be only indirectly associated with accounting per se. The proper design of forms for recording transactions, for example, assures that they are authorized, the purpose is stated, circumstances adequately described, amounts properly recorded, all forms accounted for, and names of participants or firms recorded. An example of a line level of auditing is a properly designed cash register that allows customers to observe (audit) the amounts entered by the cashier. Store display counters, security personnel, and gates and fences serve as controls to assure that merchandise leaving the premises has not bypassed the transaction recording controls. Many such business systems exist to assure that a proper accounting for all resources takes place. Making sure that these systems are used and are effective is a part of auditing.

Other kinds of audits may appear from time and time, and should not be confused with accounting audits. An operations audit is a review of the adequacy and effectiveness of functions such as computer centers, production processes, marketing activities, and so forth. A management audit is a review of managements' functions, activities, and policies. A legal audit may review contract arrangements, compliance with various laws, and other matters. A safety audit may review records of accidents, work rules, and safety features of various buildings, machines, and transport systems. A newcomer to the list is the environmental audit, which examines the emissions of air, water, noise, waste, and other impacts of the firm on its neighbors. The board should, of course, be involved in sanctioning such audits and reviewing results, just as they are involved in accounting audits.

A financial audit is generally required annually in business and many public organizations. Business corporations are required by law in the state in which they are incorporated to make their books open to inspection by stockholders. This is usually accomplished by the issuance of an annual report that includes financial statements. The materials from the Sundstrand Corporation in the Appendix at the end of this book are taken from the annual report of that corporation. The credibility of these statements is enhanced by the inclusion of the auditor's opinion.

There are various reasons for producing audited financial statements. Some involve the requirements of tax authorities at federal, state, and local levels. Audits are usually required if the corporation's ownership shares are publicly traded on organized stock exchanges. Regulatory bodies such as the Securities and Exchange Commission, public utility commissions, the Interstate Commerce Commission, the Federal Trade Commission, and others may require audited reports in filings and cases that come before them. Audited statements are often required if the firm is a member of a trade association. Bankers, brokers, lenders, and insurance companies may also require audited statements. In short, the audit of financial statements by certified external auditors is a dominant factor in almost all private and public enterprises.

THE AUDIT COMMITTEE OF
THE BOARD OF DIRECTORS

The audit committee of the board of directors represents the board as a whole in the ongoing oversight and control provided by the auditing function. This committee is instrumental in the selection of the accounting firm that is to conduct the audit, the negotiation of a contract and price, the determination of the scope of the audit, and in establishing a reporting date. It should also receive the auditor's final report and discuss identified problems and weaknesses for further inquiry. In addition, the committee should review all internal audit functions and reports. The committee should keep an open line so that internal auditors can have direct access to the committee should management attempt to override accounting and administrative controls, restrict audit activities, or suppress audit findings. A listing of audit committee duties and responsibilities identified in a typical directors' guide includes:

- Assuring the adequacy of internal accounting controls
- Monitoring the effectiveness of the internal audit function
- Recommending, selecting, retaining, and, when necessary, terminating or replacing the independent auditor
- Reviewing the auditing plan and other related services
- Receiving the audit reports and financial statements
- Overseeing the firm's compliance with the 1977 Foreign Corrupt Practices Act and disclosing audit services and committee member information required by the Securities and Exchange Commission
- Reporting on committee activities to stockholders in annual reports[2]

The U.S. District Court of the District of Columbia imposed a more formally defined legal role in one case, which provides a more definitive set of conditions and duties:

The audit committee must be composed of at least three outside directors and is authorized to:

- Retain or dismiss independent and internal auditors.
- Consult with the independent auditors on their quarterly reviews of financial statements.
- Review all monthly corporate and division financial statements and the auditor's management letter.
- Receive quarterly reports from independent auditors on internal control deficiencies.
- Review and approve all reports to shareholders and the SEC before dissemination.[3]

The growth of audit committees of boards of directors can be seen in figures published by the Conference Board. In 1967, only 19 percent of manufacturing companies and 31 percent of nonmanufacturing firms (sample of 753 companies) had such committees of the board. In 1972, 45 percent of 855 companies surveyed had audit committees. By 1978, 97 percent of member companies represented in the American Society of Corporate Secretaries reported having an audit committee.[4]

The Securities and Exchange Commission has long been a proponent of corporate audit committees. It strongly recommended the creation of audit committees in its comments on the McKesson-Robbins fraud of 1939, and further has promoted committees composed of outside directors. In 1979 the SEC issued a Release proposing rules for statements by management and independent accountants concerning internal accounting controls. It states, in part:

> The role of the board of directors in overseeing the establishment and maintenance of a strong control environment, and in overseeing the procedures for evaluating a system of internal accounting control, is particularly important. The Commission has often stressed the importance of audit comittees to enable boards of directors to better fulfill their oversight responsibilities with respect to an issuer's accounting, financial reporting and control obligations.[5]

ARRANGING THE AUDIT

Audits are relatively easy to arrange. The board of directors must of course be on record in the minutes of the board as approving an audit and the accounting firm that is engaged. The minutes of the board meeting as recorded by the secretary should show a duly made motion, a second, and appropriate vote with a quorum present. The details are often worked out by the audit committee in consultation with management.

Representatives of one or more CPA firms may be invited to submit proposals to the audit committee involving the kind of audit to be done, the areas to be audited (the scope), the time schedule, and the proposed fees to be charged. The scope of the audit is a primary factor and should include:

- The purpose of the audit plan
- The procedures or methods to be followed in carrying out the audit
- Reports to be generated by the audit
- Proposed staffing of the audit team
- Locations to be visited for audit
- Any exclusions from the scope
- Areas of special concern (to the committee or the auditors)
- Special or additional audits, if the committee deems them advisable
- Assurance that audit procedures will be in accordance with generally accepted accounting principles
- Division of responsibility between outside and internal auditors
- Budgeted cost of the audit activity[6]

Generally, proposals will take into consideration the quality of the internal audit department and the reliability of the internal accounting and administrative controls and systems. If there are doubts or perceived weaknesses in these areas, the public accounting firm will feel compelled to propose a more comprehensive examination, at higher fees. Additionally, as the actual audit proceeds, uncertainties may arise that will require additional audit investigation procedures. The final fees may be well above the initial price should these problems occur.

When the above matters have been negotiated, the auditor submits an engagement letter that formally spells out the arrangements made and the responsibilities of the auditor. Once engaged, the auditing firm selected is usually retained for an extensive period of time. U.S. firms tend to continue existing audit engagements with a single firm unless there is some dissatisfaction with the auditor or another firm demonstrates that it can provide superior services. In other countries, it is more common to rotate auditors periodically in order to assure auditor independence.

Auditors must maintain independence as a condition of following codes of ethics subscribed to by public auditors. This means that there can be no condition such as membership on the board, holding of company stock, or business dealings with the firm that may compromise the auditor's freedom to conduct the audit and comment on operations without other considerations interfering with the process.

THE CONDUCT OF AN AUDIT

An audit team will visit most of the operations of a client. They will observe the way in which the firm is organized, how goods are manufactured, or services to customers take place, the way in which inventories are received, stored, and moved through the organization, the process for keeping employee time and pay records, and a wide range of other activities. In the case of sales, they will select customer accounts at random and mail verification letters in order to check on the accuracy of receivables balances.

Auditors will examine the accounting transaction records and selectively trace the paperwork flow that culminated in the accounting entry. For example, if a purchase of 1,000 items for a sales department or for use in production is recorded, auditors will examine the paperwork trail involving purchase requisitions by the user, purchase orders and price negotiations by the purchasing department, shipping documents, receiving reports by the warehouse, routing slips, inventory records, checks issued for payments, and any correspondence on delays, complaints, returns of goods to vendors, and other records. They may also examine policies and procedures relating to internal accounting and administrative controls and verify whether operations are in compliance with the system design.

The auditors should be given the authority to access all areas of operations and any documentation necessary to carry out the audit adequately. This may include not only transaction records, but the minutes of the board of directors, general correspondence, contents of safe deposit boxes, or other types of evidence needed to support representations on financial statements. The independent auditor should also have access to the organization's attorneys and legal counsel. If some operations are not accessible, such as overseas branches, the audit report of another firm may be accepted for forming an opinion on those operations. This fact would be noted in the scope portion of the opinion. On occasion, some operations may not be open for audit, such as secret defense production plants. The opinion would note such limitations on the audit.

Not every transaction can be subjected to the detailed investigation illustrated above. Thus the auditor may use sampling techniques to assure a representative selection of matters to be audited. If the auditor finds a well-designed and fully operating system including good internal controls, the size of the required samples will be small. If serious errors are found within a sample, such as inventory transactions, the auditor may conclude that the records cannot be relied upon. He or she may then broaden the sample and include more items in order to determine the extent of the problem. In serious cases the auditor may qualify the audit opinion, noting the areas of uncertainty, contingency, or lack of reliability within the financial statements. In extreme circumstances, an adverse opinion, stating that the financial statements are not fair and cannot be relied upon, may be issued.

THE AUDITOR'S CERTIFICATE

Upon completion of the audit, the auditor formally expresses an opinion in the form of an audit report or certificate. A typical audit opinion is shown in Figure 4-1, using the Sundstrand report as an example. A more detailed report of the audit results upon which the opinion is based, called the management letter, is presented to the audit committee and to management. It is more specific as to what was done, what was found, what is recommended, and what needs to be done to make statements more reliable and assure that they fairly present the financial results for the period.

Figure 4-1 represents a "clean" opinion. It contains two paragraphs: one on the scope of the audit and one expressing the auditor's opinion. The scope paragraph indicates whether the audit was performed in conformity with generally accepted auditing standards. The opinion paragraph states whether management's representations contained in the financial statements are in conformity with generally accepted accounting principles.

The director should note that an audit is intended to provide reasonable (but not absolute) assurance that the financial statements, taken as a whole, are free of material misstatements, either deliberate or unintentional. The audit includes a study and evaluation of the organization's accounting system and internal controls. Tests of selected balances and transactions focus on significant areas and probe for weaknesses in the organization's way of doing things. It is not a complete check on everything and it is not a guarantee of the complete accuracy of the financial statements or the absence of fraud. However, if the audit is carried out according to professional standards and techniques, it is highly probable that any material financial fraud or mismanagement will be un-

Figure 4-1
The Auditor's Short Form Report

GRANT THORNTON
Accountants and
Management Consultants

Board of Directors and Stockholders
Sundstrand Corporation

   We have examined the consolidated balance sheets of
Sundstrand Corporation and Subsidiaries as of December 31, 1986
and 1985, and the related consolidated statements of earnings,
changes in financial position and stockholders' equity for each of
the three years in the period ended December 31, 1986. Our
examinations were made in accordance with generally accepted
auditing standards, and accordingly included such tests of the
accounting records and such other auditing procedures as we
considered necessary in the circumstances.

   In our opinion, the consolidated financial statements
referred to above present fairly the consolidated financial
position of Sundstrand Corporation and Subsidiaries at December
31, 1986 and 1985, and the consolidated results of their
operations and changes in their financial position for the three
years ended December 31, 1986, in conformity with generally
accepted accounting principles applied on a consistent basis.

Chicago, Illinois
February 6, 1987

covered in the due course of the audit. If fraud is suspected, a much more extensive and costly plan for the audit is necessary.

At the culmination of the public audit, it is usual for the auditor to write a management letter. This letter may discuss deficiencies found, problems that should be addressed by management, or other matters. It may contain certain recommendations to correct potential problems or weaknesses in the systems of the firm.

Many CPA firms also perform management advisory services (MAS) functions similar to those called consulting services by management firms. The management letter may seek to assist management in dealing with minor operational problems as a routine part of the audit. In the case of more extensive problems, the auditor may advise further work with professional consultants or MAS providers. If the CPA firm also is engaged for MAS work, care must be taken to maintain the independence of the auditors. The board and/or the audit committee should also meet with the auditors, review the management letter, and be involved in any contracting for these other services.

Any departures from the clean opinion as shown in Figure 4-1 should be taken very seriously. Phrases such as "except for..." or "subject to..." signal areas of auditor disagreement or major uncertainties that directors should seek to address. The presence of an additional paragraph in the opinion should be closely scrutinized. It may merely present additional information, in which case the report is still a clean or "unqualified" opinion. On the other hand, the extra paragraph may express certain reservations or unresolved situations on the part of the auditor, in which case the opinion should be considered as qualified. Qualified opinions noting irregularities or significant contingencies are likely to have an important impact on the firm's stock performance, its ability to borrow, or the kind of credit terms it can arrange with lenders.

INTERNAL AUDIT RESPONSIBILITIES

Internal audits are only slightly different in technique as compared to public audits. Internal auditors often are influential in designing the accounting systems and controls used in the organization. Internal auditors are on the scene on a continuous basis. Transactions can be audited as they occur, mistakes and errors can be found and corrected before they become a major problem, and controls can be monitored and updated on a frequent basis. Internal auditors do not customarily issue formal reports or opinions on their work.

If accounting policies or general operating policies of management are being violated, appropriate levels of authority should be apprised of the problems. If problems revealed by audits persist and no effort is being made to correct them, the internal auditors should approach the audit committee directly. Oversight and control are questionable if the directors' only source of information is channelled through management.

THE FOREIGN CORRUPT PRACTICES ACT

In the 1977 Foreign Corrupt Practices Act of the United States, a new section was added to the Securities and Exchange Act of 1934. Section 13 (b) (2) concerns the "accounting provisions," which carry a significant mandate for directors and officers of publicly held companies falling under the provisions of the act. This section requires that

(2) Every issuer which has a class of securities registered pursuant to section 12 of this title and every issuer which is required to file reports pursuant to section 15 (d) of this title shall—

(A) make and keep books, records, and accounts, which, in reasonable detail, accurately and fairly reflect the transactions and dispositions of the assets of the issuer; and

(B) devise and maintain a system of internal accounting controls sufficient to provide reasonable assurances that—

(i) transactions are executed in accordance with management's general or specific authorization;

(ii) transactions are recorded as necessary (I) to permit preparation of financial statements in conformity with generally accepted accounting principles or any other criteria applicable to such statements, and (II) to maintain accountability for assets;

(iii) access to assets is permitted only in accordance with management's general or specific authorization; and

the recorded accountability for assets is compared with the existing assets at reasonable intervals and appropriate action is taken with respect to any differences.[7]

In response to the accounting provisions of the Foreign Corrupt Practices Act, it has become a common practice to include in the corporation's annual financial report a Management Report in addition to the auditor's certificate. This report for 1986 by Sundstrand Corporation is shown in Figure 4-2.

Figure 4-2
Management's Report to Stockholders

Management's Report

The management of Sundstrand is responsible for the preparation and presentation of the consolidated financial statements and related financial information included in this Annual Report. These have been prepared in conformity with generally accepted accounting principles consistently applied and as such include amount based on estimates by management. The consolidated financial statements have been audited by the Company's independent accountants, Grant Thornton.

Management is also responsible for maintaining a system of internal accounting controls which is designed to provide reasonable assurance that assets are safeguarded and that transactions are executed in accordance with management's authorization and properly recorded. Judgments are required to assess and balance the relative cost and expected benefits of these controls. To assure the maintenance of effective internal controls, management adopts and disseminates policies, directives, and procedures, selects and trains qualified personnel, establishes an organizational structure which permits the delegation of authority and responsibility, and maintains an active program of internal audits and appropriate managerial follow-up.

The Board of Directors elects an Audit Committee from among its members, none of whom are employees of the Company. The Audit Committee meets periodically with management, the internal auditors, and the independent accountants to review the work of each and satisfy itself that they are properly discharging their responsibilities. Both the independent accountants and internal auditors have free access to the Audit Committee, without the presence of management, to discuss internal accounting controls, auditing, and financial reporting matters.

(signed)
Ted Ross
Vice President of Finance
and Secretary

QUESTIONS TO ASK

Accounting systems must capture the essence of transactions and events that affect the financial status and performance of the organization. Financial status and performance are, of course, the product of human endeavor that produces the transactions and events in the first place. If higher management creates a somewhat stressful environment for other levels of management and workers, one may expect high levels of achievement and superior financial performance. On the other hand, a too-high level of performance expectation may create frustration, failure, and stress that may move people to focus on altering the measures of performance: the accounting system.

The falsification of transactions and the subversion or override of internal controls can be a major employee response to high job pressure. In recent years, the Securities and Exchange Commission has intensified its efforts to determine the amount of fraudulent financial reporting due to this newly perceived element. Fraud for personal gain is perhaps less frequent than fraud to enhance the appearance of job performance and the furtherance of personal ambition. The director may well ask management about the methods used to set standards and evaluate the performance of individuals and departments within the organization.

Directors sometimes find it difficult to be too assertive in questioning managers on the results of the audit. The entire atmosphere and protocol of a board meeting makes it difficult to play the role of critic. Board members tend to develop a genial relationship with management and an element of trust among directors and between directors and management is the norm. If a director feels that he or she cannot believe what management says, the whole process breaks down.

A headstrong management can easily render a board powerless. A board under the undue dominance of corporate officers is likely to be assuming a considerable legal risk. The review, oversight, and control functions of the director are a legally prescribed role and failure to properly execute the role is a violation of law as well as of public trust. A board that diligently pursues the oversight and control functions has little to fear in a legal sense.

How, then, to question management on subjects revealed by audits, both public and internal? One may take the following perspective. Financial statements constitute in most cases the principal information received by the board. Audits provide additional information relating to financial statements and the organization. The board member cannot be faulted for asking for more information if financial statements and audits reveal inconsistencies or problems.

An accusatory tone of voice is a poor way to start. Rather, one may ask, for example, "The auditors question the value of certain items shown in the inventory account, Mr. Jones. What do your people in Sales view as the prospects for these products?" And again, "Has anyone done a market analysis or an economic study to back up these forecasts?" "Why do the auditors disagree with this result?" "Are we still making or buying these items?" "What steps are being taken to promote or advertise this product?" "When do you expect the disposal of these items to be completed?" If real problems exist, a manager answering such questions will in all probability begin to recognize them, and so will the board members.

In other questions, the review of the audit report should include some attention to matters such as:

- Did the scope of the audit as it was carried out differ significantly from that set forth in the engagement letter?
- Did the auditors have the complete cooperation of corporate staff and management people, and were all documents and information requested made available?
- Were any significant errors, discrepancies, or problems discovered that were referred to management but not included in the audit report? What recommendations were made to management?
- Did management respond to the recommendations made?
- Are the statements accurate and complete and are there any qualifications in the auditors' opinion certificate?

NOTES

1. Mark Stevens, *The Big Eight* (New York: Macmillan, 1981), p. 2. The big eight firms are: Arthur Andersen, Arthur Young, Coopers & Lybrand, Deloitte Haskins & Sells, Ernst & Whinney, Peat, Marwick, & Mitchell, Price Waterhouse, and Touche Ross.

2. No uniform prescription of duties and responsibilities has been adopted. This list is adapted from Deloitte, Haskins and Sells, *Audit Committees: A Director's Guide* (New York, 1979), p. 12.

3. Reported in Deloitte, Haskins and Sells, *The Week in Review*, 79-44, November 2, 1979, p. 1.

4. Jeremy Bacon, *Corporate Directorship Practices: The Audit Committee*, Report No. 766 (New York: The Conference Board, 1979), p. 54.

5. Robert K. Mautz and Robert D. Neary, "Corporate Audit Committee—Quo Vadis?" *The Journal of Accountancy*, October 1979, p. 87.

6. Bacon, p. 19.

7. Mautz and Neary.

CHAPTER 5

THE INTERNAL FINANCIAL MANAGEMENT AND REPORTING STRUCTURE

This chapter turns from matters relating to financial accounting (reporting to third parties) to the subject of management accounting (internal accounting and reports to management). While financial accounting is subject to rules and generally accepted accounting principles imposed by those outside the firm itself, managerial accounting is not so closely circumscribed. Any information, analysis, or reporting format that is useful to those making business decisions is accepted.

The underlying data base for management accounting may consist largely of the same accounts and systems designed for financial accounting. The management accountant is often responsible for both the preparation of financial accounting statements and the preparation of reports for management use. The viewpoints differ sufficiently, though, to make it desirable to separate the two reporting functions to some extent.

The National Association of Accountants has defined management accounting as follows:

Management accounting is the process of identification, measurement, accumulation, analysis, preparation, interpretation, and communication of financial information used by management to plan, evaluate, and control within an organization and to assure appropriate use of and accountability for its resources. Management accounting also comprises the preparation of financial reports for non-management groups such as shareholders, creditors, regulatory agencies and tax authorities.[1]

Internal financial management and reporting basics can be approached in three broad topic groupings: (1) management accounting and cost concepts, (2) cost accounting systems and reporting, and (3) planning and budgeting processes. The topic of planning and budgeting is presented in Chapter 6.

COST CONCEPTS

Management accounting serves many users of accounting information and must therefore attempt to organize cost and revenue data in various ways. Costs and revenues can be related to plans, product lines, organization units, management responsibility, the behavior of costs in relation to activities, and/or to any classification basis that is meaningful to managers. There are four fundamental cost concepts that are helpful in viewing the essentials of the management accounting role in organizations: full cost, cost responsibility, cost variability, and differential cost.

Full Cost

The concept of full cost means that an attempt is made to associate all product- or service-related costs to products or services produced. Some costs, such as materials and labor, can be traced directly to the creation of a product or service. They are thus direct costs and can be identified with the attainment of a cost objective such as meeting the needs of customers. Other costs, such as rent, depreciation, and staff services, are indirect in that no obvious direct association of the work performed to a particular product or customer service can be seen. Such indirect costs must be allocated to products and services produced during the period when the indirect activity is taking place. For each product or service, full cost is the total of direct costs and some reasonable proportion of indirect costs of the organization. This means that unit costs can vary depending on how many units were produced during a reporting period. This is discussed further under the cost variability heading. Generally accepted accounting principles require that full costs must be used for financial statement purposes. Federal antitrust laws require that the pricing of products must be sufficient to recover the full costs of production to avoid problems of unfair competition.

Cost Responsibility

The managerial concept of cost responsibility relates to the organization structure. When a cost is incurred to create a product or service, it is possible to identify the responsibility for the amount of cost to a person, a department, or a planned or budgeted activity. For example, if labor costs in Department A are $62,000 in the production of Product X while the plan was to spend $60,000 the difference can be identified for reporting purposes as the responsibility of: (a) Department A, (b) Joe Smith, the Department A supervisor, or (c) the Product X manager. It may even be that the responsibility is that of the Personnel Department, which may have allowed a wage increase.

A fundamental assumption of responsibility accounting is that costs should be reported in management reports at the level where the ability to control the cost can be identified. The process of identifying the real cause and responsibility for costs can be difficult. The incurring of excess materials cost, for example, might be due to changing prices paid by the purchasing agent; the excess use or waste of material due to labor inexperience, faulty machinery, or machine setup; or the poor quality of materials delivered by the vendor.

At higher organization levels, reports of cost differences are aggregated under successively higher levels of responsibility and become more difficult to analyze. Attention is then most usefully focused on major classes of discrepancies and actions taken to regain control of costs. To the extent possible, managerial accounting reports should provide some analysis of the major problems identified in the area of responsibility.

Cost Variability

The cost variability concept concerns the fact that costs tend to vary in relation to the volume of products or services produced. Management accounting attempts to identify elements of cost by their behavior in relation to volume. The basic structure of costs includes some costs such as direct materials and direct labor that vary with the volume of production, and other costs that remain constant or vary disproportionately with production volume. It is important in planning and budgeting and in managerial analysis to understand this structure of costs. The formula that illustrates cost behavior is simply that total cost is equal to fixed costs plus the variable cost per unit times the number of units produced. A common expression of this relationship is:

$$TC = a + b(x)$$

where a is the fixed cost in dollars, b is the variable cost per unit, and x is the number of units produced.

To illustrate, assume that fixed cost is $6,000, direct material required per unit of product is 1 pound at $5 per pound, and direct labor required per unit is 1 hour at $7 per hour. If 1,000 units are produced:

$$TC = \$6,000 + \$12 \,(1,000), \text{ or } \$18,000$$

This amounts to a unit cost of $18,000 \div 1,000$, or $18.

Should the production level rise to 1,100 units instead of 1,000, fixed costs would not be expected to change and total cost will be:

$$TC = \$6,000 + \$12\,(1,100), \text{ or } \$19,200$$

The cost per unit is now $19,200 \div 1,100$, or $17.45. The difference is due simply to the fact that more units were produced and each absorbed or was allocated a proportionately smaller amount of fixed cost. The effect of production volume and the structure of cost on cost variability can be a powerful planning, measurement, evaluation, and control instrument. This concept is discussed further in the material on break-even analysis later in this chapter.

Differential Cost

The fourth managerial accounting concept, differential costs, refers to the basic premise that some costs will be different under each alternative course of action being contemplated. It is only those costs that will be different that are relevant in making comparisons and choices. An analysis of cost differences is important in many management decisions. Assume that a choice is being made between continuing to manufacture a product in-house using resources that are in place, and the opportunity to contract out or have manufacturing done by someone else. (This is often referred to as a make or buy decision.) In this case there will be no differential revenue. The same number of units will still be made and offered for sale at the same price. But what cost differences (differentials) will occur?

The obvious cost differences are the substitution of the production contract cost for outside manufacture in place of internal costs. What internal costs will be different? Clearly, the direct material and direct labor cost components will be eliminated. The fixed costs are another matter, however. If the building also houses manufacturing activities for other products, it is improbable that building rent costs allocated to the contracted product can be eliminated. Other costs may be reduced somewhat, such as computer and staff services, but probably not in proportion to the reduction in direct costs. In making the decision, management need only compare the costs that can be saved with the costs of purchasing the units from another manufacturer. Only those costs and revenues that will be different are relevant for decision making.

In accounting terms, a sunk cost is one that is irrelevant for decisions. A manager considering the sale of unneeded equipment should ignore the original purchase cost of the equipment and the annual depreciation charges based on that cost. Only the current resource flows—selling price and/or cost savings resulting from the sale—are relevant for the decision to be made.

These four concepts form a basic frame of reference for management accounting in providing useful information to managers: full cost, cost responsibility, cost variability, and differential cost. Applications of these concepts can be seen in some aspects of management accounting analysis and reporting that follow and in the director's understanding of problems and opportunities that are discussed in the remainder of this book.

BREAK-EVEN ANALYSIS

Break-even analysis is a planning, budgeting, and evaluation tool that addresses the basic cost structure of the organization. While breaking even is not ordinarily a business objective, it is important under some circumstances to know the dollars of sales or the number of units of product sales that are required to cover all costs. Further, the picture of the structure of costs that is provided in this analysis is an important planning and decision-making model.

Let's bite the bullet at this point and look at a few numbers that help illustrate this method of analysis. At the core of break-even analysis is the contribution margin provided by the sales of the product. In a previous illustration, direct material costs per unit of $5 and labor costs of $7 were incurred in the manufacture of a product. Fixed costs were $6,000. If we now assume a unit sales price of $25, it can be seen that the sale of one unit of product produces a contribution of $13 ($25 - $12) toward covering the $6,000 of indirect costs that are fixed in total. The sale of 462 units ($6,000 ÷ $13) will just cover indirect and direct costs and allow the firm to break even. Expressed in dollars, sales revenue at the point of break-even is 462 units at $25 per unit, or $11,550. Using our cost formula this can be expressed as follows:

$$\$11,550 = \$6,000 + \$12\,(462)$$

Another approach to break-even analysis is the contribution ratio method. The key to this method is the determination of the percentage of the sales price that is available to cover fixed costs. In our example, variable costs are $12, which is 48 percent of the sale price ($12 ÷ $25). Therefore, 52 percent of the sale price is available to contribute toward coverage of the fixed cost, or 52 cents per dollar of sales. The break-even point can thus be calculated as follows:

$$\$BE = \frac{FC}{1 - \dfrac{VC}{SP}} = \frac{\$6,000}{1 - \dfrac{\$12}{\$25}} = \frac{\$6,000}{.52} = \$11,538$$

If sales are currently at the $17,500 level, the management accountant might note that the margin of safety (the amount of sales above the break-even point) is $5,962. About one-third of sales are contributing to profits. The gross profit on $17,500 of sales is calculated as follows:

$$\begin{aligned}
\text{Profit} &= \$25\,(x) &-& \quad (\$6,000 + \$12\,(x)) \\
&= \$25\,(700) &-& \quad (\$6,000 + \$12\,(700)) \\
&= \$17,500 &-& \quad \$14,400 \\
&= \$\ 3,100
\end{aligned}$$

Management decisions frequently involve investments in new plant and equipment and the expansion of services such as advertising and computers. The resulting increases in fixed costs tend to raise the break-even point and thus decrease the margin of safety. Unless sales are increased, profits decrease. Where the new fixed assets or services decrease the variable costs of production, it is possible to offset the investment and increase the profitability of sales past the break-even point.

Assume that an additional fixed cost per period of $1,000 is incurred in order to increase labor productivity so that $5 of labor cost per unit is required instead of $7. The contribution ratio is increased to 60 percent and the break-even point is relatively unchanged as can be seen below:

$$\$BE = \frac{\$6,000 + \$1,000}{1 - \dfrac{\$10}{\$25}} = \$11,667$$

The amount of gross profit, with the level of sales unchanged, is now $3,500, calculated below:

$$\begin{aligned}
\text{Profit} &= \$25\,(700) &-& \quad (\$7,000 + \$10\,(700)) \\
&= \$17,500 &-& \quad \$14,000 \\
&= \$\ 3,500
\end{aligned}$$

The $1,000 added fixed costs have in this example added $400 per period to gross profits.

The break-even analysis can be extended to setting sales goals to produce a desired profit. If a $2,000 profit is desired, the sales level must be at the point where the contribution margin will cover both the fixed cost and the desired profit. In formula form:

$$\$S = \frac{\$6,000 + \$\ 2,000}{1 - \dfrac{\$12}{\$25}} = \frac{\$8,000}{.52} = \$15,385$$

The number of units of sales required is $15,385 divided by $25, or 615 units.

The example is now extended to accommodate a management goal of a $2,100 profit after taxes. We assume that the fixed costs include all organization period costs as well as the fixed manufacturing costs. The tax rate on income is assumed to be 30 percent. It can be seen that the profit goal of $2,100 represents the 70 percent of profits left after deducting the 30 percent tax liability. Profits before taxes are thus $2,100 divided by .70 or $3,000, and the required level of sales is:

$$\$S = \frac{\$6,000 + \dfrac{\$2,100}{1 - \text{tax rate}}}{1 - \dfrac{\$12}{\$25}} = \frac{\$9,000}{.52} = \$17,308$$

The company in the example has current sales of $17,500 and will therefore exceed the profit goal of $2,100, because it requires sales of only $17,308 to meet the profit objective.

An advantage of the contribution ratio approach used in the above illustrations is that the contribution ratio can be calculated using either unit sales price and variable cost or by using total sales dollars and total variable costs. If several products are involved, an overall sales level can be determined, but the makeup of individual product decisions is obscured by the use of the total sales and dollar figures. It is useful as a general assessment of a company's position and to observe the effect of investments in assets or activities that change total fixed costs.

A rudimentary knowledge of break-even analysis, coupled with the perspective of the cost structure of the firm that it gives, can permit a greater involvement of directors in the consideration of proposed courses of action.

ORGANIZATIONAL DECENTRALIZATION AND ACCOUNTING

Many organizations are run from the top. Management tends to be authoritarian and business objectives are not communicated very well to subordinates and workers. A small firm or one that utilizes very simple technology, in limited markets, and under an experienced management, can function well under a centralized management structure. Even a high technology firm with a homogeneous range of products under an expert manager may find management from the top to be advantageous. Centralized management can digest information quickly and initiate rapid responses to changing circumstances.

However, when the firm is large, operating in multiple technologies, with differentiated nonhomogeneous products, conducting operations in multiple markets, and/or with limited executive experience in these areas as a whole, decentralization of management may be essential. Management decentralization is not the same as physical dispersion. A firm may have several widely dispersed manufacturing or sales operations and yet be closely managed by a centralized management. The term *decentralization* is usually used to describe a management philosophy of decentralized or autonomous decision making. To overcome the circumstances described above, decision-making authority may be delegated to various divisions or administrative units that are expected to act as independent business entities. Authority over these units is thus lodged in the people most knowledgeable about and closest to the activities being directed.

In exchange for the autonomy and decision-making authority granted to division managers, controls are generally imposed by the home office or headquarters management group. Divisions are after all still expected to contribute toward the goals of the whole organization and act rationally to enhance the interests of the stockholders.

Controls over divisional performance in decentralized organizations generally center on accounting information and management policies that are expected to influence division managers in a positive way. A common accounting control, for example, is to establish a return-on-assets goal that is expected of the division by the home office. A policy control might stipulate that equipment expenditures larger than a certain dollar amount must be approved by the central finance function. It is common to impose on decentralized divisions certain personnel, promotion, and pay scale requirements, the use of a prescribed chart of accounts for accounting purposes, and other operational guidelines. The division manager is largely left free to determine production, inventory, sales volume and pricing, and other aspects of management direction. Such controls have the benefit of being indirect and not requiring a high level of technical expertise of the decision maker. They can also increase the level of satisfaction of the division manager.

If autonomous divisions buy and sell products and services to each other, disputes may arise as to the proper transfer price for these goods and services. In centralized organizations such transfers are made at cost and the accounting system merely accumulates costs as goods move about. In decentralized units treated as profit centers, however, the accounting entry recording a transfer to another unit of the organization must reflect the profit one would expect of a sale to parties outside the organization. At times, disputes arise between buying and selling divisions about the appropriate transfer price.

While these issues do not generally involve the board of directors, they may produce irritations among managers that can surface in other ways. Management accounting often involves fact-finding and special analyses to help managers arrive at an acceptable and independently negotiated transfer price arrangement. In examining internal reports on divisional performance, the director should understand and weigh the possible transfer price effect on the profits reported. This is especially critical in the evaluation of foreign operations where the transfer price may serve some other purpose as well. This topic is discussed in greater detail in Chapter 11.

NONROUTINE DECISIONS

The majority of business decisions concern ongoing and routine activities of the organization. Production, personnel, research, sales, purchasing, finance, and other functional departments are usually created to provide specialized management over these basic activities. Accounting usually serves a scorekeeping purpose and maintains an attention-directing focus with respect to such essential activities that must be done well to assure long-term success for the enterprise. Both financial and managerial accounting are involved in scorekeeping and attention directing. A third accounting aspect is problem solving, and management accounting is the dominant arm of accounting here.

In addition to its involvement in routine operations and decisions, management accounting plays a primary role in what might be termed nonroutine decision situations faced by managers.[2] These might include decisions on such matters as: whether a product should be manufactured by the company or purchased from independent sources (make-or-buy), market strategies and pricing, manpower planning, capital spending, business expansion, new products, product abandonment, distribution channels, whether to own assets through outright purchase as opposed to leasing them (lease/purchase), and other nonroutine questions. The director's role of providing review, oversight, and control in these areas is essential. The analyses generally made by management accounting and managerial finance people should be readily available to directors when such nonroutine decisions are to be made.

COST ACCOUNTING SYSTEMS

The central role of costs in business and not-for-profit decisions, and the tracking of the flow of costs through the organization, were illustrated in Chapter 2. All resources are obtained through sacrifices measurable in terms of cost. The costs of various inputs are reflected in transactions between the firm and unrelated outside parties. This may seem to be a simple matter of record keeping, but various business practices may obscure even this computation. As resources are used or combined to manufacture products or carry out various other activities, costs become even more problematical.

Consider the cost of materials used in manufacturing a product as an example. A catalog or list price may be $250 per unit of the parts or materials, and 100 units are ordered. The cost is apparently $25,000. However, the status of the buyer in the market may entitle the firm to a trade discount of 20 percent, a quantity discount of 2 percent, and cash discounts or terms of 2/15, n/60 (a 2 percent discount on the invoice amount if cash payment is made within the first 15 days of the 60-day credit period). The cost of this purchase is thus $19,110, not $25,000. The calculation is made as follows:

Purchase (list) price	$25,000
Trade Discount (20%)	(5,000)
Quantity Discount (2%)	(500)
Invoice Price	$19,500
Cash discount on payment (2%)	(390)
Final price paid on order	$19,110

The unit cost is thus $19,110 ÷ 100, or $191.10, not $250. If two of the 100 units acquired are lost in the manufacturing process or emerge as scrap worth $50, what is the unit cost of the materials used in manufacturing? The purpose of the cost accounting system is to accommodate circumstances such as these and produce cost figures useful for management and for an acceptable financial reporting of inventory and cost of goods sold.

Three major cost groupings are present in any manufacturing or construction endeavor, as has been discussed previously. The first is the cost of raw materials, parts, and subcomponents that form the finished product. These are referred to as materials. The second cost grouping is the wages earned by direct factory labor. This category includes all amounts paid to workers whose efforts are directly expended on the physical product as it moves through the manufacturing workplace. These costs are termed labor. Together, direct materials and direct labor are called prime costs. The third group of costs, referred to as conversion costs or overhead, is a mixture of factory operating costs such as supplies used, utilities, salaries or supervisory personnel, clerks, warehouse personnel, drivers, maintenance workers, rent, insurance, depreciation on factory buildings, and so forth.

Figure 5-1
Manufacturing Cost Flows in Accounting

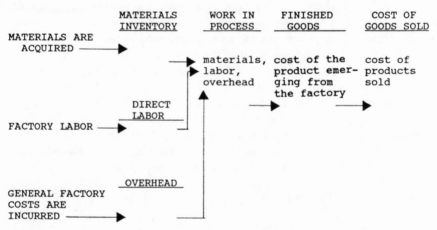

Figure 5-2
The Statement of Cost of Goods Manufactured

```
                       X CORPORATION
            STATEMENT OF COST OF GOODS MANUFACTURED
                FOR THE MONTH ENDED 5-31-Y8


Work in Process 5-1                                          $ xx

Materials
    Materials Inventories 5-1                    $ xx
    Add Purchases of Materials                     xx
    Materials available                          $ xx
    Deduct ending inventory of materials        (  xx )
    Materials used during the month              $ xx

Factory Labor                                      xx

Manufacturing Overhead Applied                     xx
Total Manufacturing Cost                                       xx
Total work in process for the month                         $ xx
Deduct work in process at end of month                      (  xx)
Cost of goods transferred to finished goods                 $ xx
Add finished goods at beginning of period                     xx
Deduct finished goods at end of period                      (  xx)
Cost of goods sold                                          $ xx

(Possible adjustment for under/over applied
    overhead to reflect full costs may be shown.)           $ xx
```

As the fabrication and assembly of products takes place, the costs of materials, labor, and overhead are brought together under the classification "work in process." This accounting procedure parallels the actual work of bringing materials, labor, and services together on the factory floor.

When the production process is completed, the product is moved off the factory floor and stored until it is shipped out to the distribution system. Similarly, the accounting procedure removes the accumulated production costs from work in process to a finished goods inventory account. The ultimate sale of the product is reflected in the cost accounts as a transfer of cost from the finished goods inventory account to the cost of goods sold account. All costs determined to be factory- and production-related inevitably follow the process described above, which is summarized in Figure 5-1. These accounts are reported in a Statement of Cost of Goods Manufactured, usually available only to internal personnel and not a part of the public reporting process. Figure 5-2 illustrates the format of a typical manufacturing statement.

Two types of work in process accounting are in general use, depending on the nature of the production methods and products: job order costing and process costing. Where manufacturing takes place in a continuous movement of a relatively homogeneous product through various stages, or a series of departments, costs can be accumulated by department and assigned proportionately to all products emerging from the process. Examples of this type of process production are an oil refinery or a home appliance manufacturer. Process costing thus accumulates the costs of materials, labor, and overhead by departments or processes and then reallocates the total costs to the quantity of products emerging from the process.

Job order costing systems accumulate the material, labor, and an allocation of overhead costs to each unit or batch of products moving through production. A plant may make a variety of products, each with a unique manufacturing specification, such as a machine shop or automobile assembly plant. Each unit or group of products requiring a particular production pattern can be "costed" by keeping track of the costs of specific materials used and direct labor hours expended, and allocating overhead on some basis such as labor hours.

Some manufacturing firms use a system of standard costing to simplify the accounting process and to tie product costing to cost planning and budgeting and control documents. When incorporated in the accounting system (standard costing), the end-of-period cost reports will disclose cost variances. These variances reflect the use of more or less than the standard cost of the three cost factors of materials, labor, and overhead. They quickly draw management attention to areas where costs are not following the standard. Variances detail the effects of paying more or less than the standard for materials and labor, the effects of producing more or less than the planned level of output, and the incurrence of more or less than the budgeted overhead costs.

Manufacturing variances, usually no more than about six or seven numbers, can provide directors with an effective monitoring of the pulse of the firm's operations. These are seldom available to those outside the firm. Variances generally tend to reflect unplanned results and help to pinpoint responsibility. For example, if materials prices rise, a material price variance will result. The purchasing office may be asked to explain. Should sales prices then be raised? Marketing people should be consulted. If a material quantity variance arises, it may signal a process in trouble: high spoilage or waste, errant equipment, or poorly trained workers. Variances are also presented in the budget reporting system, and budget variances can serve the same purpose of disclosing areas of revenue and spending that may need review.

Short-term differences between what was planned and actual results reported are always with us. The longer the period covered by the financial reports, the more likely it is that a variance is indicative of a real problem. Studies have tended to show that quarterly reports are about the right frequency for higher levels of management and for directors.

More frequent reports tend to include the effects of short-term variables that are not really out of control. As the time for reporting approaches, people in the organization are working to achieve the expected results—reach the production, or spending, or sales plan, for example. Too-frequent reports require an inordinate amount of effort in catch-up activities. For example, a plan to produce 60,000 units in the 60 working days of the first quarter of the year does not mean that exactly 1,000 units per day or 5,000 units per week are to be expected. Managers have the discretion, over the three months, to accommodate the many factors that keep output from being so exact. Good operating people will achieve the objective, but are happier if they can do it their own way and at their own pace. Most people in offices and industry are well aware of the end-of-period concentration of activity to reach an objective.

Quarterly variances thus will tend to reflect real operating problems rather than the timing difficulties that shorter-term reports show. Firms that operate under highly seasonal factors may not be on target until the whole year is finished. Consideration should then be given to developing reports keyed to seasonal expectations each quarter rather than expecting one-fourth of the year's planned activity, revenue, or cost.

Some directors and officers prefer reports that show only the variances and omit the actual figures for results and the budget or plan details. Simply reporting variances in dollars and percentages is seen by such people as sufficient to note problems and form a basis for questions. Once a plan is accepted, it is only the variances that should be a subject of concern. This approach is not common in most firms, but it does reflect a no-nonsense view that quickly identifies where the time of an officer or director can be most productively spent.

SUMMARY

This chapter has described some basic aspects of managerial accounting and cost accounting, which form the basis for the internal accounting and reporting structure. The managerial accounting concepts of full cost, cost responsibility, cost variability, and differential costs were described. These concepts were then illustrated in applications such as break-even analysis, organizational decentralization, and nonroutine decision making. Finally, the basic nature of costs and the accounting and reporting systems employed was described. While cost analysis and reporting is not the function of the director, the understanding of cost data and its use in operations review, oversight, and control *is* the directors concern.

Much is heard about cost planning, cost containment, cost control, cost reduction, and cost effectiveness in business and government. Yet one must realize that costs merely reflect the financial effect of what people and organizations do. Costs do not change unless there are changes in the underlying activities that costs classify and measure. Cutting the planned expenditures by 10 percent cuts the amount available quite effectively. But what activities will be reduced or eliminated in the process? That is the real domain of cost cutting. It is important to understand the structure of costs, in that only variable costs can be effectively reduced. Those costs that are fixed may in fact account for a large part of the total. In that case a 10 percent total cost reduction may impact variable costs in a much larger percentage, since only variable costs can be affected by current decisions. Each choice of what activity to curtail or eliminate will have effects on the organization and its environment. The possible effects are often only dimly perceived by those who mandate the cost reduction.

It is easy to cut expenditures for advertising, or research, or maintenance, or clerical positions in a business, or for a school district or public library. The real cost of such changes may far exceed the money saved in the short run. Such economic or social costs do not appear on the organization's financial reports in the current period, but are real nevertheless. Money saved by improperly servicing equipment is likely to be more than offset by future equipment replacement costs. Cost control should focus on those activities that incur the highest economic and social costs if they are not done properly. Cost reduction or elimination can focus on areas that will have the least short- and long-term effect. This topic is discussed in Chapter 10.

An area of accounting called social accounting has developed as an accepted accounting discipline to bring out the associated nontransactions costs and benefits of decisions made in the boardroom and in the plant, but social accounting has not achieved wide popularity or use. For the present, the director should cultivate an intrinsic feel for the wider implications of the concept of cost.

NOTES

1. National Association of Accountants, *Statements on Management Accounting*, No. 1A (March 19, 1981), p. 4.

2. Lawrence A. Gordon, Danny Miller, and Henry Mintzberg, *Normative Models of Managerial Decision Making* (New York: National Association of Accountants, 1975).

CHAPTER 6

THE DIRECTOR AND
THE BUDGETING PROCESS

A budget is a document that lists the expected revenues and costs for activities during a given time period. In almost any survey of top management, budgeting ranks as the dominant instrument and process for planning, coordinating, communicating, controlling, and evaluating the organization's activities. The budget document itself is an explicit elaboration of organizational commitments for the period, and it reflects the resolution of demands for resources and expected performance attainments by units and by functions within the organization.

The budget itself is created in the management process of arriving at a planned level of activities and results for the period. The need to achieve a desirable overall financial result expressed in terms of the budget leads to people blaming the budget for all sorts of perceived problems when activities fail to attain the planned objectives. The budget has been blamed for imposing stress on people, for causing managers to become department-centered rather than people-centered, for causing other unpopular management practices, for limiting the flexibility and creativity of people, and numerous other problems.

In any organization, the question is not whether to have budgets but, rather, the degree of formality to be given to them. If they are not formal—that is, in written financial form and derived from a structured budgeting process—they may exist only as implied managerial and supervisory expectations for sub-ordinates. Between the formal and implied, one may find extensive operations performance requirements and standards but without the translation into finan-cial terms. To be successful, however, an organization must at some level of management have a financial expectation that is based on the costs and revenues associated with what it does: in other words, a budget.

Budgeting is not really an accounting process. Rather, it tends to reflect many basic managerial responsibilities that might be interesting from the perspective of the review, oversight, and control functions of the director.

Among the operational and budgeting responsibilities of management are:

- to *forecast* or anticipate what is going to happen
- to *plan* activities consistent with the firm's environment
- to *budget* resources to enable the plan to be carried out
- to *implement* plans through people and the organization structure
- to *analyze* results in terms of appropriate measurements
- to *evaluate* the performance of people and functions
- to *control* people and activities to achieve planned results

The budget document itself is only one step in the budgeting process that includes all of the stages in the management process described above. The budget shapes the responsibilities of management into specific achievements in specific time frames. The budget may serve as a basis for the release of re-sources to effectuate the plan and as the basis for authorizing expenditures by specific individuals. A variety of budget reports are prepared at more frequent intervals within the budget period for purposes of analysis, evaluation, and control. The term *budget* refers to the budget document and related progress reports, while the term *budgeting* is used here to reflect the entire process of formulating the budget and using it in managing the organization.

The board of directors must usually examine and approve the budget and related objectives submitted by management. They should realize, however, the significance of what has happened before the final budget is documented, and what should occur subsequent to its implementation. Most budgets are prepared for an annual period of operations. Interim financial reports, those for a month or a quarter, can most meaningfully be evaluated when compared with the budgeted projections for the period. A satisfactory bottom-line quarterly income figure may disguise significant departures from planned annual opera-tions, revenues, and costs. These variations should be reported to the directors and questioned by them.

THREE MISCONCEPTIONS ABOUT BUDGETING

One encounters three major misconceptions about the nature and uses of budgets. These may be seen as mere technicalities to some people, but can lead to misunderstandings if not recognized early on.

The first misconception is that a budget is a forecast. It is not. Forecasting is the predicting of future conditions. It may include demographics, economics, politics, and consumer behavior among other scientific studies. Certainly budgets are based on such predictions. A demographic prediction of a larger proportion of middle-aged people in the population can surely influence expected figures for production, prices, wages, and other conditions.

Second, budgets are sometimes referred to as financial plans. They are not. Budgets are operating plans expressed in financial terms involving how resources are to be used and reflecting management's policies. Financial plans spell out such things as sources of capital, operations profits, investments to be made, financing arrangements, dividends, cash and credit management, inventory policies, and so forth. Budgets of course reflect these decisions and policies.

Finally, some view budgets as future decisions. They are not. All decisions reflected in the budget are current decisions made in light of expectations about the future. If activities during the period of the budget prove to be unworkable, other decisions must be made at that time to change the activity and determine the new revenue and cost implications. In budgeting, all required decisions guiding future performance must be made in the present so that anticipated resource needs and availability are recognized in the plan.

THE MASTER BUDGET

The master budget for an organization may have three major parts. The *operating* budget is based on the costs of various organizational activities and revenues they are expected to produce. The *cash* budget is based on the cash inflows and outflows of the period, their timing, and the borrowing and investing required during cash shortages and surpluses. The *capital* budget details the plans for the acquisition and disposal of long-term assets and the changes in the capital structure of long-term debt and stockholders' equity. These three budgets may be combined in what is called a pro forma statement, which is essentially a projection of the income statement and balance sheet that can be expected for a given period of operations if the master budget evolves as planned.

Of the budgets described here, the capital budget is probably the one that will occupy most of the attention of the board of directors. Operating budgets and cash budgets are more or less self-policing once they are approved. Directors are seldom able or willing to challenge management's assertions and projections based on detailed forecasts and operations plans. An acceptable bottom-line profit is probably the major criterion for a director unless large variations in the interim budget reports place the total projected profits in jeopardy.

The pro forma statements will draw some attention because of changes in the discretionary factors in the components of financial statements: inventory levels, receivables, payables, various costs and expenses, short-term debt, cash on hand, and so forth. But the capital budget represents a long-term commitment that will shape operations and financial statements for years to come.

SOME BASICS IN
OPERATIONS BUDGETING PROCESSES

Organizations whose size or complexity preclude a tightly run, top-to-bottom management style find it desirable to establish a budget committee. This committee forms a vehicle for obtaining the participation of officers and managers in the budgeting process, coordinating the budgets of all functions and responsibility areas, resolving differences, and submitting the final budget for approval. In the process, a great deal of communication, negotiation, and consensus-building occurs among all levels and areas of the business. It is here that the interpretation of the organization's goals and objectives into operational terms takes place. The committee may be composed of officers and managers with other responsibilities in the organization, or in some cases may draw some of its membership from a staff budgeting department.

It is generally desirable to create the full-time position of budget director to assure a coordinated budgeting effort and to make the responsibility for budgeting more specific. The budget director can work closely with management in the process of setting guidelines and coordinating the efforts of the budget committee. The director is a key figure in the presentation of the recommended budget to the board of directors and in responding to concerns and questions that arise.

A budget staff may be required to provide the budget committee with needed information and to relieve operating personnel of the need to divert excessive attention to data gathering, analysis, and communication during budget construction. The staff assembles forecasts for sales and develops production and inventory requirements, plans for acquisition of materials and labor, and expected expenses for the period, as well as gathering other needed data for the budget committee. This staff could be composed of specialists employed full time for budgeting, or it could also consist of operations personnel temporarily co-opted for the purpose of helping the budget committee. In some large organizations the period of time devoted to budget building may be several months.

Some argue that those involved in budgeting should be people who are experienced in the firm's operations and knowledgeable about the business. Others say that these insiders are too close to the action and too busy. They may also be unable to deal adequately with superiors and peers since they must eventually return to their former relationships. Budgeting specialists with no line responsibilities would therefore be more independent and objective in resolving problems. A good justification is possible for either view, and each organization develops its own pattern for the budgeting process.

BUDGET COMPONENTS

Budgeting for operations generally follows a sequence that starts with the sales forecast and the related expectations for the unit sales and prices of various products and services. It is useful to have some idea of the projected total market for each product and a projected share of that market for the organization's products and services. This *sales budget* and revenue plan and the required number of products then forms the basis for other budgets that are briefly explained below in their normal sequence.

The *inventory budget* is constructed in light of the sales budget. It must consider the amount of inventory carried over from the previous period of operations, the expected sales, and the desired ending inventory level of each product that will assure an adequate service to customers. This establishes the production volume required.

A *purchasing budget* is constructed in units and in dollars (and schedules for the cash budget) to meet the production volume and schedule.

A *manpower budget* is then developed given the number of workers and related skills, pay and fringe benefit projections, and necessary supervisory, training, and other costs.

Operating expense budgets detail the expenditures required for support functions, energy requirements, safety and health, utilities, insurance, sales and administration, and other areas.

To this list of budget components may be added a *discretionary expense budget*, which includes such expenditures as research, product development and engineering, advertising, education and training, and others. A *financial budget* or *cash budget* is prepared to anticipate the expected pattern of cash flows and investment and borrowing activities that will be required by the coordinated master budget and pro forma statements.

A *capital budget*, usually covering a longer time span or with a rollover factor, is often desirable for expenditures and borrowings for plant and equipment items and for basic financing arrangements. If the budgeted level of activity exceeds the capacity of the plant and its equipment, the additional capital spending must be planned and implemented. It is also imperative to maintain a desirable balance between invested (equity) and borrowed (debt) sources of capital. Long lead times are necessary for any rational approach to such long-term capital needs. In many organizations, long-range operating budgets of five or more years are constructed in order to anticipate the development of capital budgets and the sources of capital required to support expanded activities.

One can begin to see the potential for complexity and the amount of time required for the purposes of budgeting. If it is done reluctantly, in haste, or without adequate communication, planning, and information inputs, the budgeting process can fail. The budgeting process should be well planned and fully supported by directors if it is to reach its full potential of assuring coordinated, supportive, and open participation in deciding upon and reaching the organization's goals and objectives.

BUDGET FLEXIBILITY

Given the amount of effort involved in budgeting, it is common to keep to the basics and develop a single operating budget that reflects the plans for the period. The fixed budget is appealing in that all efforts are focused on the attainment of given activities within the resources planned. If revenues and costs differ from the budget, an analysis of the differences (budget variances) is useful in evaluating the organization's operations.

A problem arises when the costs of activities, such as sales, production, and supporting services, are at a level higher or lower than budgeted. Sales that are 10 percent higher than planned, for example, probably require higher-than-planned variable costs for materials, labor, and variable overhead items. The budget report thus indicates unfavorable budget variances in those cost elements. Most organizations are quite happy with higher sales levels, however, and variances in elements of cost are to be expected as the price for achieving higher revenue.

One of the major drawbacks of fixed budgets is the mixed message received by management: favorable sales levels and unfavorable cost levels, or vice versa. Another drawback is that it is difficult to assess the appropriateness of costs adequately in relation to sales even at the budgeted level, let alone at higher or lower levels of achievement than those planned. Fixed budgets have an advantage in that they remain focused on the expectations and plans for the period and portray the effect of sales and production differences on revenues and costs. This benefit is not to be taken lightly. When management misses the mark, the consequences should not be hidden, as they may be in variable budgeting.

A variable (or formula) budget is often considered more useful for analyzing and evaluating organizational performance and achieving operational control. The outward appearance of a formula budget is similar to a fixed budget. It is based on a planned level of sales, production, and support services, as is the fixed budget. The main differences are in the method for the determination of the budget amounts and the way budget reports are prepared.

The preparation of a variable budget usually requires some analysis of cost factors by their relative fixed and variable cost components. Utilities costs, for example, may be composed of a base rate plus a unit cost for usage above a given amount. The budget formula for utilities might then be expressed as:

Budget = Basic Charge + (Unit Charge × Units Used)

In the previous chapter, on cost accounting, this behavior is shown as:

Total Cost = Fixed Cost + (Unit Cost × Units)

Another example is supervisory personnel costs. At a basic production level, three supervisors may be required. As production volume rises, an additional supervisor may be required for each ten employees added. Such a cost would be called semifixed because the cost changes in chunks.

Each cost element in the construction of a formula budget is analyzed and projected on the basis of its relationship to volume. A single budgeted dollar amount results, then, for a given planned volume. At the end of each budget reporting period, however, the budget is reformulated in terms of the actual levels of activity that occurred and the dollar amount produced by the application of the formula to each cost element. The report comparing budgeted amounts with actual amounts shows variances to the extent that the cost incurred did not behave according to its expected pattern.

An advantage of the formula budget approach is that actual costs that vary from the variable budget are an indication of potential cost control problems or departmental inefficiency. If sales and production are different from the planned level, the budget figures are changed and if the formula is realistic, no significant budget variances should be reported. The budget is thus more realistic and motivates people to keep costs in line. A disadvantage of formula budgets is that budget reports do not in themselves portray the successes or failures in attaining the initial planned results approved by the management and staff and the board of directors.

A variation of formula budgeting is flexible budgeting. In this approach, more than one level of operations may be planned and budgeted. If actual results lie between two of the budgeted levels, either the nearest budget is used for analysis and reporting, or an interpolation is made to arrive at a budget for comparative purposes. For example, budgets are made for production levels of 8,000 and 10,000 units. An actual production level of 9,500 units would require adjusting all budget figures by the percentage of the difference in the results. Material costs of $16,000 and $20,000 budgeted for 8,000 and 10,000 units, respectively, would be shown in the flexible budget report as $19,000, determined as follows:

$$\$16,000 \quad + \quad \frac{(\ 9,500\ -\ 8,000)}{(10,000\ -\ 8,000)} \quad \times \quad (\$20,000\ -\ 16,000)$$

Flexible budgeting has the disadvantage of requiring people to construct two or more budgets instead of only one. It also assumes that costs are strictly variable and linear in the interpolation between two fixed budgets. It is a useful approach where costs are difficult to analyze in terms of their fixed and variable components. The report produced will have the same usefulness and problems described above for variable budgets.

SINGLE VERSUS MULTIPLE PERFORMANCE CRITERIA

Budgeting sets forth plans and costs in all major cost and revenue categories in the organization. The effect is to establish performance criteria in a great many areas of endeavor. For example, the plan on which the budget is predicated may call for the purchase of a given number of units of each material at a projected unit cost. The budget report and cost analysis at the end of the budget period may indicate both a quantity and a price variation in the final results. In this case and throughout the budget many such performance criteria (multiple measurements) demonstrate how well costs have been controlled by those responsible for operations.

It is difficult to evaluate higher levels of management using many detailed operational measurement criteria. It is common to condense the record and use more general summary analyses of performance. For example, a measure of the cost of inventory on hand as a percentage of total current assets or net sales will yield an indication as to whether inventory costs are stable, and thus presumably under control. The cost of goods sold as a percentage of total sales similarly yields a measure relating to cost control when compared to past trends or to industry averages reported by trade associations.

Multiple financial criteria and a variety of operational measures such as labor productivity, product quality, and personnel turnover can provide a basis for evaluating managerial performance in several dimensions but not in the detail that budget reports can produce. By setting goals in these broader areas, operating management is better able to balance cost and revenue and operational factors in making day-to-day decisions. Those who evaluate management's performance may be too distant from operations or not well enough informed about what each cost element should be to perform an adequate evaluation on that basis. General measures and limited multiple performance criteria thus have many advantages for directors and officers of the organization.

Even limited multiple measures of performance may be confusing, especially where the real criterion is simply to make a profit on the invested capital. By using a single performance criterion such as return on investment, all operating data are summarized in a measurement related to one overriding goal. This also leaves the manager free to decide many things with no limitations beyond the objective to be achieved.

This progression of performance evaluation criteria—from detailed multiple measurements of all components of revenue and cost in the budget, to general multiple criteria combining several financial and other attributes of the organization, to an overall single criterion—has illustrated a variety of control frames of reference. The literature on controls in organizations notes major flaws in each method. In general, evaluation criteria for managers should be clearly expressed, understood, and adhered to by officers and directors when evaluating the performance of managers and of units of the organization.

There are dangers in a single criterion because one can never be certain as to the legality and ethics of the available methods used by managers to achieve that one goal. Too many criteria may lead to short-term management performance to make the figures fall in line rather than the reach the real goals of the organization. Even in the Soviet Union, multiple performance criteria and quotas are often weighted by the individual manager according to the perceived importance and relevance of a particular major criterion (such as setting a production record) that may be different from period to period. They have even at times used profit as a single control measure for Soviet managers.

The review and oversight role of the director would appear to require more than a single performance criterion. Objectives and performance plans should recognize many of the complexities of business operations that are best controlled through a set of relevant criteria for measuring multiple aspects of performance. The operating budget provides a real opportunity for examining a great many variables and asking insightful questions.

OTHER ASPECTS OF BUDGETING

Since the budgeting process involves all aspects of management responsibility and administration, it is not surprising that it has a motivational use as well as a planning use. It is unlikely that a director would be involved at this level. However, those interested in how the budgeting process influences people may be interested in a brief closer look at budgeting.

If a budget is to motivate the achievement of the planned level of activities at the planned level of costs, it must communicate the priorities of the organization and promote coordination among organizational units such as departments or divisions. A participative budgeting process involves those responsible for performance in the construction of the budget. The give and take in working out ways to achieve desired results and determining related cost factors is the first step in gaining the enthusiasm and support of members of the organization.

Contrary to the participative budget is the imposed budget. An imposed budget, in its pure form, is constructed by the top level of management of the firm and is essentially an order to accomplish certain activities using a specified amount of cost for each. Imposed budgets are based on the idea that only higher management can set organizational goals and objectives and determine the best way to achieve them and how much should be spent in doing so. The budget thus serves as an implement of an authoritative management style. Both types of budgeting processes can yield the desired results, but each creates its own impact on employee involvement, motivation, and satisfaction. Actually, neither form is found in its purest form in practice. Some claim that all budgets are participative to some degree.

Under either concept of budgeting, another motivational factor is the extent to which the budget is based on an easy-to-attain set of activities and costs (a loose budget) or a difficult-to-attain set (a tight budget). A loose budget provides ample resources and/or low expectations of performance. Operations managers may create a loose budget by bargaining for slack. This often takes the form of asking for more funds than are necessary to do the job, or by asserting that fewer activities can be accomplished than they know are possible with the resources available. Slack allows the manager to meet problems in a noncrisis atmosphere and also to be rewarded for accomplishments greater than planned or costs lower than budgeted.

A tight budget represents a high expected level of performance compared to resources and costs allocated for the manager's use. There is little slack in the sense that only very good performance will accomplish the desired results in activities and costs. Somewhere between the extremes of tight and loose budgets is a budget that motivates good performance, rewards real accomplishment, and leads to high levels of satisfaction among employees when the budget is attained. The term *motivational* budget is used for the latter type of budgeting philosophy.

In some cases a simplified approach to budgeting is found in the incremental basis of making budget decisions. An example of this approach is to carry forward the prior period budget with an incremental change. For example, if projected sales represent an increase of 5 percent from the previous period, all costs are budgeted at a 5 percent increase as well. This approach is simple and easy to accomplish. It is usually seen as fair by those working under such budgets. However, this methods ignores increased efficiencies and economics of scale that should accompany higher volumes of activity. Each activity in the budget is assumed to be of equal value and continues to be funded regardless of changes in the need for the activity or differences in the importance of the activity in reaching organizational objectives. An incremental budget can easily be constructed in a few hours and without much effort or involvement of various levels of management.

At the other end of this budget spectrum is the zero-base budget approach. In its pure form, each activity planned must submit a justification for its continued existence, explain its purpose, its past achievements, and new activities to be undertaken. A list of priorities is also required so that the lowest priority items can be examined in competition with other such programs for the best utilization of available resources. In effect, each activity and its costs compete at a basic level each year for its continued existence. Because of the time involved in yearly preparation of budgets, individual programs may undergo a zero-base assessment only every four or five years. In the interim, they may be budgeted on an incremental basis. A form of this approach is to authorize and fund activities for only a set number of years. The activity's authorization and funding automatically expire at the end of that time unless a justification can be made for the continuation of the activity. This is sometimes referred to as a "sunset" provision. In practice, zero-base budgeting has not proved to be workable in most cases because it is a costly and lengthy process, encourages infighting among organization units, and introduces complex political agendas into budgeting deliberations. Popular activities might be listed as low-priority items so that it would be risky for executives to allow the termination of the function.

GENERAL CONSIDERATIONS

Budgeting tends to become a more formal process under any of three conditions. The first is when top-level management is no longer able personally to plan, coordinate, supervise, evaluate, and control operations. Management begins to lose touch as the organization grows and more people and products and markets are involved. Second, when there is a high degree of technology, innovation, or instability in the organization's environment, more specialized knowledge and expertise is required. The few at the top begin to experience drifting and inability to make informed decisions. Thus, financial evaluation becomes a valuable tool for planning, decision making, and control in place of the personal observation of activities.

Finally, if a firm becomes decentralized and operational responsibilities are delegated, financial controls such as budgets permit a continued forum for top-level involvement in decision making. Decentralization may occur for reasons given above, or to meet geographical separation of organization units or a broader customer base (consumer versus industrial sales, for example), or any of a number of reasons.

Budgets should be viewed both as goals and constraints, but also on a more positive note in the sense that they also perform an enabling function. Any activity worth doing (providing benefits and profits and opportunities) can find its way into the budget. In addition, budgeting sales and production for 100,000 units should not be viewed as a constraint that prevents the production and sale of 120,000 units if the added activity is feasible and promises to produce favorable financial and strategic results. Far from prohibiting or impeding the creativity of members of the organization, budgeting permits the competition of ideas in a neutral forum that keeps the goals of financial success and survival at the forefront.

ACCOMMODATING CHANGE

Studies on the frequency of management reporting have suggested an optimal reporting period of three months, or quarterly. This allows a smoothing of short-term cost and marketing variations and yet permits controls to assure progress toward objectives. A problem facing any leader is the need to change plans as circumstances warrant. A leader who changes plans and circumvents disaster is applauded and expands his or her number of followers and supporters.

However, a leader who changes plans too often, or at the slightest hint of trouble on the horizon, can be seen as indecisive, fearful, and a hindrance to orderly processes of organizations.

A change in the budget during the period of operations should be viewed as an extraordinary and rare event. Changes create confusion, doubt, lack of coordination, new relationships, and insecurity unless carefully made. If the old budget is clearly in error or has been based on faulty forecasts, or is otherwise unworkable, by all means it should be changed and the executive should work hard to show the necessity for change and direct the new effort. In many cases it may be best to communicate the expected problems to those affected and give them a chance to innovate or accommodate the change and still reach the objective. Respond to the problem, but do not change the budget! Accommodating the problem may be easier than the effort to enter an unexpected budget revision process at the same time. Of course there will be budget variances if the problem causes a change in activities and costs, but the budget report will now chronicle the extent of the financial effect of the problem and its resolution.

Even in warfare, one would think that constant changes in the order of battle are the rule. But leaders such as Adolf Hitler and Dwight Eisenhower seldom changed complex strategies, despite new information that increased the risk of the plans. They depended on the ability of their people to meet the challenge, and they avoided the appearance of waffling and delaying in the making of crucial decisions.

Figure 6-1
Use of Standards and Budgets for Control

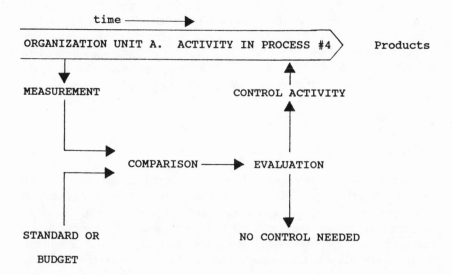

A summary view of the role of budgets and performance standards and criteria is illustrated in Figure 6-1. The activities of a given unit of the organization are depicted moving toward an objective such as the manufacture of a product, providing a service, or marketing products and services. Periodically, a measurement of some attribute of the activity is made. This could be costs, revenues, labor hours, material usage, number of accidents, labor turnover, or other measured attributes. The obtained measurement is compared with the budget, standard, or any management expectation. If the difference (variance) is minor, the evaluation may point to doing nothing: the activity is under control. If the variance is large enough to place in doubt the ability of the unit to meet its goals, the evaluator may initiate control activity to modify the errant performance.

One of the advantages of management decentralization and the participative use of budgets as controls is that much of the process described above and in Figure 6-1 is self-contained and almost automatic in each area of operations. The budget report comparing measured performance with the standard or budget can be assumed to provide a strong motivation on the part of the manager to determine the causes of variances and to take steps to correct problems. He or she does not have to be told that there is a problem and how to correct it. Higher levels of management do not have to investigate and analyze department operations and determine an appropriate corrective activity. Only when the on-the-scene manager is unable to handle the problem in a reasonable time frame is there a need for higher management involvement.

These controls are effective because of the budget or standard and the psychological need of all of us to be successful and perform our duties well in terms of the measurement criteria used. Whether a budget is imposed or participative, if the performance criteria are reasonable and attainable, they will bring forth the energy, creativity, and loyalty of people to meet the budgeted goals. To paraphrase a noted philosopher, be careful in setting your goals and ambitions, for you are likely to achieve what you want. The golden touch of Midas illustrates goals gone awry.

CHAPTER 7

THE FUNCTIONS OF THE TREASURER AND THE CORPORATE CONTROLLER

The financial aspects of business performance are generally associated with the expertise of two functions: treasurership and controllership. Generally, more is known about the treasurer's duties than those of the controller. The corporate director should interact frequently with these officers.

Every corporation *must* have a treasurer. This position is a fundamental responsibility spelled out by laws in all states. A chairman, a secretary, and a treasurer must be listed in the articles of incorporation, and certain duties and reports are generally prescribed for each. These positions may be elected by the board of directors or by the stockholders at large, in the manner prescribed by law or in the bylaws of the organization.

Every corporation *should* have a controller. There is no legal requirement for this position, nor is there a fundamental responsibility prescribed with the office. The controller does not *control* in the active sense of the word. He or she cannot give orders or accept line responsibility without jeopardizing the effectiveness of the position. The controller is one who provides and analyzes information that should be made available to management in planning and running the business.

THE TREASURER

The treasurer is the chief financial officer of the organization. Responsibilities include the operation of the accounting system, the issuance of financial reports, the raising of capital to finance operations, the employment of capital in investments and operating assets, the payment of interest and principal on funds borrowed, reporting to various tax and regulatory bodies with jurisdiction over the organization's financial affairs and operations, and other duties. He or she is responsible for the controls that assure both the protection of assets and their use for duly authorized purposes of the organization. An accepted set of functions for the office of treasurership has been set forth by the Financial Executives Institute (FEI).[1] The seven areas of responsibility and the author's discussion of each are presented below.

Provision of Capital

The treasurer is to establish and carry out programs for providing the capital required by the business. This responsibility requires the selection of sources of capital and the negotiation of terms and other financial arrangements. The term *capital* as implied here includes all sources described as liabilities or owner equity. The emphasis, however, is usually on long-term financing sources such as debt issuances (bonds and mortgages) and the sale of equity securities (shares of the firm's stock).

The process for obtaining capital on a long-term basis is long and complex. A two- or three-year period of planning and execution before funds are actually received is not uncommon. The treasurer becomes familiar with lawyers, bankers, securities analysts, credit rating agencies, and investment bankers and brokers, among others.

The corporate director is generally kept informed of the organization's capital needs and the potential sources of funds by the treasurer. The board, of course, must vote approval of such longer term financing contracts and arrangements by the treasurer. A subcommittee of the board may be appointed to consider financial matters as they arise and to assure proper oversight for this function. The finance committee would report to the full board in the event major proposals are put forth.

Investor Relations

The FEI prescribes that the treasurer "establish and maintain" an adequate market for the organization's securities. He or she is, as a part of that responsibility, to maintain an adequate liaison with investment bankers, financial analysts, and shareholders.

Organizations do not approach capital markets on a routine or frequent basis. These are major decisions and carry major commitments for the organization. Once having issued securities, however, frequent attention is required. If a security is performing inadequately, such as an erosion of market value for the organization's stock, the treasurer should determine the problem and attempt to deal with it. Stock prices tend to decline if the earnings of the organization are low or if the degree of perceived risk is high. Obtaining operating efficiencies in cost control, and in developing product pricing strategies, may be the first steps in correcting such a problem. It is of course management's responsibility to initiate actions to correct cost and pricing problems.

The treasurer should assure that news of the organization's successes or of favorable future prospects reaches the investment community. Contacts with managers of institutions such as pension funds, insurance companies, and investment funds may persuade them to purchase and include the organization's securities in their investment portfolios. Records of holders of bonds and stocks must be carefully maintained. Dividends, interest, and sinking fund payments must be on time and follow the overall strategy of the organization. Contractual provisions must be followed, such as maintaining a required cash balance, current ratio, or relationship between debt and equity on the Statement of Financial Position.

Short-Term Financing

The treasurer is to maintain adequate sources of current borrowings from various lending institutions. Cash inflows and outflows rarely coincide in the course of business operations. In times when cash needs are great and insufficient cash is currently available, the treasurer must depend on creditors and commercial banks for the cash to meet the temporary shortage. A variety of arrangements are possible, such as a short-term unsecured note for a month or two; the flooring of inventories, whereby the bank pays the creditor and is repaid when inventories are sold; a line of credit arrangement allowing the firm to overdraw its bank cash balance temporarily or to cover quickly the shortage through automatic borrowing as needed. The factoring or sale of customer receivables also offers short-term cash availability.

In most cases, short-term financing arrangements are not subject to board of directors approval. The board may well retain control in this area by setting limits on short-term borrowing. It may, for example, require approval of selling accounts receivable, or short-term borrowing beyond a dollar total of, say, $50,000. If restrictions are established, the board should empower its finance commitee to authorize exceptions to its policies in real financial exigencies unless a quorum of the board can be called on very short notice. Financial exigencies should be a rare event for most organizations.

Banking and Custody

The treasurer is to maintain banking agreements; to receive, have custody of, and disburse funds; and to have similar responsibilities with respect to securities. The financial aspects of real estate transactions are also the treasurer's responsibility.

The handling of cash is probably the weakest link in the safeguarding of assets, because ownership of cash is difficult to prove. It belongs to whoever has it. It is at this point that a treasurer's responsibility for accounting systems seems most critical. Cash coming into the system—customer sales cash and checks, proceeds of short-term borrowing, payments mailed in by customers and others—must be recorded in the accounts and immediately separated from transaction documents and deposited in the bank. Records of cash bank deposits each day must be checked against recorded cash sales, customer payments on account, and cash collections on other accounts. Any discrepancies must be investigated. Any problems with customer balances, bank overdrafts, uncollected notes, or loan records must be monitored.

All cash disbursements should be made by sequentially numbered checks. A reconciliation of cash balances on bank statements and on the books of account should be done monthly. Checks should be signed by authorized individuals and numerical amounts should be unalterable. Check vouchers should indicate the particulars of the payment: to whom? for what? Payments involving unfamiliar names or suspicious organizations or an inadequate explanation of the purpose of the payment should be examined.

It is not necessary here to go into the detailed controls of funds of the organization. However, the auditors and the board should receive assurance that controls and procedures are in place, are working, and have been tested. For example: Where is the safe? Who knows the combination? Who is responsible for closing the safe at 5 o'clock? What papers must be kept in the safe overnight? Who locks the office? Who turns on the alarms? Has someone written the safe combination on the wall behind it? (This is not a foolish question!) How often are door locks changed? When an employee is discharged or quits, who collects keys, badges, and identification cards? Who arranges for a change of combinations and locks when there is an employee turnover? These are just a few policy matters dealing with controls in only one small area of operations.

The treasurer is responsible for the issuance of securities and other debt instruments upon approval of financing plans by the board of directors. He or she should maintain records of names of stockholders and transfers of ownership, and disburse dividends to the proper stockholders upon approval of the board of directors. These functions are sometimes carried out by an independent trustee who supervises the interests of both the stockholders and the organization. Similarly, bonds held by registered bondholders require maintaining bond registration lists and assuring that bond interest payments are on time. Funds must also be provided for paying bondholders who hold unregistered bearer bonds when they present interest coupons for payment.

State and federal securities laws must be followed to the letter in all applicable areas when issuing stocks and bonds, when making the contracted payments, when recalling or repurchasing securities, and when settling accounts at maturity. If the bond contract (indenture) requires an appropriation of retained earnings or the creation of a sinking fund to repay the securities at maturity, such provisions must be honored.

There may be provisions in some cases that require the corporation to maintain a stipulated relationship in the financial statements, such as a 2.5:1 current ratio, or a 4:6 debt/equity ratio. A violation of these types of covenants may have serious consequences for the corporation, such as the immediate maturity of the debt.

The organization may have employee stock option plans, bonus plans, savings plans, pension plans, and health plans that the treasurer helps negotiate and administer. All of these must be authorized by the board of directors, with subsequent oversight and control as the treasurer administers such plans.

Most organizations have real estate interests that fall under the custody and protection duties of the treasurer. Many real estate holdings also involve mortgage loans that are significant debt, interest, and repayment obligations of the corporation. The treasurer is responsible for timely tax and insurance premium payments related to real estate holdings. In addition, the treasurer should ascertain the necessity of holding various pieces of property and dispose of those that have little or no potential use. If such property is leased to others, additional related administrative duties fall on the treasurer.

The organization may lease property, plant, and equipment from others. In such cases, the treasurer must assure that an accounting system that meets generally accepted accounting principles for leases is in place. Certain contractual commitments may also accompany a leasing arrangement and the treasurer must supervise these requirements.

It can be seen that the banking and custody responsibilities of the treasurer are a continuous and detailed process that enables the firm to carry out its day-to-day operations.

Credits and Collections

Granting credit and collecting accounts owed to the organization constitute a fifth treasurer responsibility. Sales to customers often involve special financial arrangements, sometimes including special terms of sale or time payment contracts. In addition, sales of high-cost durable goods may take the form of leasing arrangements in which only the services of the product are sold, not the product itself.

An adequate system of credit granting, transaction recording, account classification, customer billing, and the follow-up of delinquent accounts should be provided under the treasurer's supervision. In the case of installment sales, interest should be accounted for according to generally accepted accounting principles and reported separately in a manner that distinguishes income from selling goods and services from that relating to interest.

The treasurer should provide for the daily deposit of amounts received from customer collections into appropriate bank accounts. Periodic checks of customer balances should assure that payments have been recorded and that balances are correct. Customers have little tolerance for errors in billing. Policies should also guide such areas as when to write off accounts as uncollectible, what collection efforts should be undertaken, reporting to credit agencies, and so forth.

Organizations dealing with expensive, long-lived products such as automobiles, airplanes, machinery, and buildings may rent or lease these items to customers. Sometimes a lease contract may cover the effective useful life of a product and thereby represent a sale with payments to be received in a manner similar to an installment sale agreement. Accounting rules require distinguishing an operating lease or rental arrangement from financing or lease purchase, which is to be treated as an installment sale under accounting rules. In establishing leasing policies, the treasurer should adequately consider the appropriateness of various types of leases and contractual provisions.

Accounting rules for leases require treatment as a lease purchase if any of the following situations apply:

- The lease transfers ownership of the property to the lessee
- The lease contains a bargain purchase option
- The term of the lease is equal to 75 percent or more of the estimated economic life of the leased property
- The present value of the minimum lease payments equals or exceeds 90 percent of the fair value of the leased property.

There should of course be some assurance that the lessee is able to make the required payments, and that there are no major uncertainties concerning future costs to be incurred by the lessor in connection with the assets leased to others.

Investments

As the organization accumulates funds beyond current needs, the treasurer is to seek appropriate investment opportunities. In addition, the FEI suggests that the treasurer establish and coordinate policies for the organization's pension funds and other trusts. The objective in these cases is to earn interest on these funds as well as to protect them.

Funds become available to organizations from a variety of sources, and seldom is there an exact matching between funds received and the internal funds needs of the organization. Excess funds develop from time to time and for long as well as short periods of time. Short-term excess funds may occur when seasonal product sales and the manufacture of these products are at different times. Large firms may invest cash balances for periods as short as a weekend.

When funds are to be accumulated for longer term uses such as bond redemption funds, contingency reserves, equipment replacement funds, or pension funds, the treasurer usually becomes involved in long-term investments such as U.S. Treasury notes, corporate securities, or trust arrangements that place the funds under professional management for safety and adequate return. In all cases, the treasurer must seek an appropriate degree of safety of various investments, a maximum rate of return on investments, and the availability of funds to the corporation when they are needed for internal purposes.

Insurance

The seventh of the FEI-prescribed duties of the treasurer is to provide insurance as required. Insurance requirements vary widely in most organizations. Included may be health insurance for employees, safety and liability insurance, product liability insurance, casualty insurance on properties, and employee life insurance plans. Bonding for employees who have cash and property custody responsibilities (surety bonding), and performance bonds for some kinds of contracts may also be a part of the insurance responsibility of the treasurer.

The treasurer is responsible for selecting insurance agents or firms, negotiating the policy agreements, and assuring that conditions are met. Fire insurance policies, for example, may require periodic inspections, extinguisher and sprinkler systems, systems tests and evacuation plans, and certain administrative policies on flammable waste accumulation and disposal. The administration of social security insurance, state and federal unemployment insurance, and other such insurance deductions and deposits are usually under the treasurer's responsibility.

A Comment

The position of treasurer is a legally prescribed corporate office and function, as was noted at the beginning of this chapter. In this sense, the seven areas of responsibility identified by the FEI and briefly discussed above are understood to be basic legal responsibilities of the board of directors. The review and oversight function of the board is critical in these areas. The treasurer should routinely report to the board on any problems and the current status of financial affairs. The board should seek assurance that good policies are in place and are working as they are described. This is also an important function performed by the auditors. It may be quite interesting for board members to look at the auditor's checklist of areas to examine and questions to ask. These matters go far beyond the perusal of financial records and reports.

THE CONTROLLER

The controller may best be described as the information officer of the organization. The controller is increasingly seen as the analyzer and interpreter of financial numbers. He or she is a problem-solver who zeros in on trouble spots and works with management to identify alternatives and make informed decisions. He or she keeps an eye on where the organization has been, where it is, where it is going, and perhaps helps management decide where it ought to be going. The controller is usually a central figure in planning, budgeting, and performance reporting and analysis.

The controller's expertise generally stems from a working familiarity with accounting systems and a knowledge of the operations of the organization. He or she must also develop good working relationships and communications with managers and officers. When important decisions are being made, the controller should be there to give advice on the economic feasibility of various proposals. The Financial Executive Institute, formerly the Controllers Institute of America, has identified seven important areas of controllership involvement.[2]

Planning

The controller is to develop a plan for the control of operations and establish this plan as an integral part of management. Included in this area are sales forecasts, cost standards, expense budgets, profit planning, programs for capital investing and financing, and establishing procedures for putting the plan into effect. To some, this area of responsibility sounds like management itself. However, it is the controller's role to see to it that these planning and control aspects of management are carried out "as an integral part of management." The controller is to aid management, not to become management. Being involved in these central management activities, the controller often has the broadest grasp of the total scope of activities and is instrumental in management presentations to the board of directors and to stockholders.

Reporting and Interpreting

The controller is to ensure an adequate accounting system to measure financial performance, compare results with operating plans, and interpret the results of operations to various levels of management, the board of directors, and the owners of the business. This responsibility includes the formulation of accounting and reporting policies, the coordination of reporting systems and procedures, and the preparation of operating data, financial reports, and special reports as required by management and by law.

The controller is not responsible for the results being measured and reported and is thus in a unique position to provide an honest, unbiased reporting system. So important is this unbiased feedback that decentralized organizations often provide divisional controllers who are to provide the functions above to profit center managers. The success of the division is thus also the success of the divisional controller.

Special reports are often required by management for a variety of purposes such as union wage and hour negotiations, commercial contract negotiations, pension plan administration, executive bonus plans, and legal defenses in product pricing, product warranty issues, labor wage issues, and other adversarial issues.

Evaluating and Consulting

The controller is to serve as a consultant to all levels and areas of management responsible for policies and actions in the organization. As these policies and actions relate to the structure of the organization, its procedures, the effectiveness of operations, and the attainment of objectives, the controller's analysis, evaluation, and advice are vital.

In the busy and complex process of making decisions and delegating functions and authority, managers may not have the luxury of stepping back to see if the whole is better than the sum of its parts. The controller can develop this more comprehensive view and consult with management to coordinate and improve operations, policies, and procedures. One of the advantages of organizations is, in elementary terms, that two people working together can do more than the sum of each person working alone. The term for this is *synergy*. The controller can help in assuring that this efficiency is achieved.

Tax Administration

Tax policies and procedures must be formulated and integrated into management decisions. Tax reports and tax payments must be accurate and timely. These are relatively easy. More complex is the structuring of management decisions to assure compliance with tax laws and also to minimize the liability for taxes. Tax law complications include the wording of contracts, the dates on which certain events occur, and the accounts to which cash is posted and from which payments are made.

Government Reporting

An important aspect of controllership is the preparation of increasingly numerous reports to municipal, state, and federal governments and regulatory agencies. Antitrust laws, environmental protection laws, labor laws, securities laws, consumer protection laws, pension laws, product liability laws, pollution laws, laws governing international trade and commerce, and tax laws mentioned above are but a few of a myriad of reports with which organizations must contend.

Many groups compile statistics on business performance, such as trade associations, state commerce departments, federal bureaus and agencies, and credit agencies. Questionnaires and reports of a wide scope are received and should be completed and returned on a timely basis. These may not seem directly related to controllership in all cases, but the responsibility for assuring the timely preparation and submission of various reports often falls on the controller. In some cases serious penalties are the possible result of a failure to comply with external reporting requirements.

Protection of Assets

Traditional functions required to protect assets include the proper accounting treatment and classification of assets, internal control, internal auditing, and assurance that adequate insurance coverage exists. Some areas that the controller sometimes enters in providing protection are of interest. The proper placement of equipment and their appropriate maintenance and repair; the provision of alarms, security personnel, fences and secured areas, and personnel safety devices and activities may find their way into the controller's jurisdiction.

Two more fundamental responsibilities of management stewardship are sometimes described as the protection of the owners' investment and the responsibility to increase that wealth through the wise employment of the organization's resources. In a sense, this list of controllership areas reflects the controller's responsibility to help management keep these responsibilities at the forefront.

Economic Appraisal

This last of the seven controllership areas defined by the FEI is perhaps the most difficult; it may also be the most arguable. This responsibility is to appraise economic and social forces, including governmental influences, and to interpret their effect upon the business. Organizations come into contact with economic and social forces on many fronts. The purchasing agent in the quest for good sources of supply at the best cost, the sales department seeking the appropriate selling price, the personnel department negotiating wage rates, the treasurer seeking sources of long-term funds—all are in contact with economic forces on a daily basis.

Social forces are less direct. Clothing and food fads, consumer attitudes about corporate citizenship, population movements, demographic changes in age, income, family size, home ownership, and so forth are difficult to assess in terms of their effects on the organization. The controller may not be in the best position to make such interpretations.

Predicting and interpreting governmental influences on the organization may be risky business indeed. Tax, investment, commercial, and social legislation are undeniably strong influences on organizations. Those who follow emerging issues and trends are sometimes successful in predicting and interpreting, but only the largest organizations seem able to afford people to do this on a full-time basis.

Again, however, the FEI suggests the function. The controller may in fact be the most effective in seeing to it that others seek out the available knowledge.

It should then be made available for interpretation and communication to those who can effectively integrate such knowledge in the decision process. A good part of such information may already be incorporated intuitively by individual managers and need only be formalized and communicated to others.

Certainly the budgeting process provides an appropriate forum for bringing together information that was previously scattered so that the planning process can be more integrated. As each part of the organization assesses its own future in response to economic and social forces, there is a need to share information, coordinate plans, and achieve the best distribution of resources within the organization. The controller facilitates this cooperative effort within the structure of goals and objectives of the organization as a whole. The budget for the period is the culmination of a great cooperative effort and sharing of information of all types throughout the organization.

A Comment

There is a cliché that "information is power." That is, those who have more access to information than others are in a position to influence others through the selection of the amount, timing, and form of the information to be shared. At lower levels of the organization it is specialized information that gives those with education and experience the ability to supervise and guide subordinates. At higher organization management levels, the importance of specialized information gives way to more general and integrative information. Setting goals for the future and assessing organizational performance in the present require large amounts of general information. Not knowing the full extent of the information used by higher management, few subordinates are in a position to fully assess or challenge the roles they are assigned or the achievements expected of them. Figure 8-4 in the next chapter presents a brief look at the relationship of the amount of information to its volume and level.

The controller stands at the juncture of a great many sources of information and must integrate such sources as a part of his or her function. The opportunity for power—the impulse to make the decision—is there and must be avoided if the controller is to be effective. Some writers in the 1960s and 1970s predicted, and found examples of, the assumption of line or decision-making authority by controllers. Fortunately, controllers resisted the temptation or wisely changed jobs to become line managers and executives themselves. Controllership should remain an information-based function for the benefit of management at all levels.

An advertisement for a recent controllership position seems to capture the essence of the function:

You'll be a key participant in the operation of the company by providing accurate financial data, and preparing business plans and recommendations to the department executives. Directing the activities of Accounting, Financial Analysis, Order Processing, and Management Information Departments, you'll establish, coordinate and administer a plan for controlling the operation of business plans. In addition, you will be involved in the preparation of forecasts, the annual audit, and protection of company assets....[3]

CONTROLS AND CONTROL

The term *control* is generally used in the active sense: exerting one's will or design upon another. It may also represent a state or condition to be achieved, such as being in control or having things under control. Control is the direct sense of the term. It is often equated with power, influence, authority, or perhaps subjugation or dominance. It may even be seen as manipulation: control over others without their knowledge or willing consent.

Control in the active sense is well established as a historical and legitimate right of the governors over the governed, the leaders over the led, and the manager over the subordinate. There is a concomitant term or definition that has received less prominence in literature but has been equally significant in the historic sense of government, leadership, and management. That term is *controls*. Controls are indirect, have fewer negative connotations, yet are equally effective in achieving the ends of organizations and groups. Controls are the plans, systems, and procedures to be followed and the knowledge of the objectives toward which plans are directed. In short, information is the basis for organizational controls.

Members of boards of directors have few if any opportunities to exert control over the operations of the organization. They operate most effectively by establishing controls. That is, they approve plans consistent with objectives and desired accomplishments, they receive information about results, and they hold management responsible for adhering to plans and achieving what was expected. To the extent to which people know in specific terms what is expected of them, receive information (feedback) about measured results, and direct their efforts to overcoming obstacles and achieving desired results, controls are effective. They operate without the use of power or direct control by one person or group over others.

Recall an earlier expression of the control model, in which control is seen as a function of goals, processes, and constraints. Controls operate in the domain of the first two factors. If goals are seen as important and worth striving for, subordinates will do all in their power to do their part in achieving them. In this case, active control over the specific activities by which goals are achieved is replaced by indirect controls that focus on the objectives to be reached. Similarly, if the process for doing the work is highly structured or has built-in constraints that do not permit a departure from the design of the system, control can be indirect. Some lack of freedom and suppression of innovation will be felt, but the system will operate without the direct control or constraint of the leader imposing instructions and sanctions on subordinates.

As an information function, controllership is instrumental in any system of controls. Budgeting provides the basic plan of operations and communicates the plans and relevant financial aspects to participants in the organization. Accounting systems record financial events, measure performance in financial terms, aggregate measurements by budget categories, and provide feedback to those responsible for each budgeted area of performance. If measured results are inconsistent with planned results, operations management can be alerted to problem areas in terms of costs or revenues, and the controller can help in analyzing causes of problems and areas of needed management attention. Authority and power are not at issue in the process. It is achievement and problem solving that are highlighted.

Accounting controls, in addition to providing measurement and feedback, may also structure the processes by which actions are guided and kept under control as an integral part of operations. As an example of process controls, consider the purchase and use of materials and products in a merchandising organization. Various departments submit purchase requisitions: requests for needed materials and products. The purchasing department chooses a vendor who can offer the best price, quality, and on-time delivery and issues a pre-numbered purchase order. As goods are delivered to the receiving department, a receiving report is prepared showing what was delivered, its quantity and condition, and a comparison with shipping documents. A comparison of the purchase requisition, purchase order, receiving report, shipping documents, and vendor invoice is made and the transaction is recorded in the inventory and accounts payable accounts. There is little opportunity in this process for employees to take inventory items for their own use, or for cash to be paid without services being received. Control in this case is based on controls: a structured process and communication and built-in checks on the operation of the system. Supervisory control need only assure that employees follow the prescribed systems.

It is interesting to note that the Foreign Corrupt Practices Act of 1977 requires that the board of directors and management ensure that controls are in place and that they are used as intended. A reasonable assurance that controls are in place and adequate is generally provided by the outside auditors. Any weaknesses pointed out in the annual audit should be corrected as soon as it is practical to do so.

Three essential components of controls have been presented: (1) a structure of goals and organizational purposes and objectives that are understood and accepted by all participants, (2) an organization structure and policies and processes that limit the opportunities for people to depart from prescribed ways of doing things, and (3) constraints in the form of supervisory action and direct intervention by management when problems are found.

Some combination of the above three elements of controls should be present in all organizations, though a greater emphasis on one or two of the three may be appropriate. Where work is highly structured, such as most routine work in offices and factories, process controls can provide a high level of control. Goals and constraints may be minimal elements of control.

In some cases such as marketing and research, few process controls or supervisory constraints are effective, and a reliance is placed on *goals* in the control environment. Emphasis is placed on the importance of the work, the team approach, professionalism, the satisfaction of achievement, and the recognition of individual accomplishment. Not-for-profit organizations often must seek controls through the emphasis on goals and the importance of organizational success. Churches, relief organizations, youth groups, and governmental social services are examples of organizations with goals as a major control ingredient.

A constraint basis for control may be required where unskilled labor must be used, where goals cannot be communicated in a form that attracts loyalty and effort, or where adequate process controls cannot be used. One would expect a greater use of supervisory personnel and detrailed instructions as a basis for work performance. Sanctions and penalties or short-term bonus or reward systems may be required in this control form.

Goals and process controls are based on establishing the purpose and goals of the organization, the structure by which the work is to be accomplished, and adequate communication among people. The controller can be instrumental in providing the structure and in assuring the free flow of plans and performance information that highlights goal achievement. Little formal feedback is normally provided to workers where constraints constitute the only effective control means.

CONCLUSION

The roles of the treasurer and the controller have been discussed in this chapter. The position of treasurer is a legally required one in corporations, while the controller's office is discretionary. The functions of each officer as promulgated by the Financial Executives Institute have served as the basis for the discussion and expanded upon. The nature of control and controls has been developed here to underscore the positive nature of indirect-, information-, and systems-based controls that underlie the controllership role.

The board of directors relies on the information and reports produced by the treasurer and the controller more than they may realize. These officers are important in developing and maintaining the effectiveness of the president and managers of the organization. Their presence at board meetings can often afford insights on the problems and prospects of the organization.

NOTES

1. "Controllership & Treasurership: Modern Definitions," *Financial Executive*, June 1964, pp. 49–50.

2. Ibid.

3. Information Access Company, Recruiting advertisement in *The Wall Street Journal*, April 21, 1987, p. 48.

CHAPTER 8

THE WORKING RELATIONSHIP BETWEEN DIRECTORS AND MANAGEMENT

The leadership of business organizations is provided by the chief executive officer. A common title for this position is president. In a formal sense, the president is elected or appointed by the board of directors and has a direct responsibility to that group. The board of directors, in turn, is elected by and is responsible to the stockholders. In some cases the CEO may have a title like "executive director" if he or she is also a board member. The board often elects a member to serve as chairman of the board of directors. Two additional official positions on the board are the treasurer and the secretary and these positions are generally required by state law. Their duties are usually further spelled out in the corporate bylaws.

The election of directors is accomplished by a vote of the common stockholders who have one vote for each share of stock owned. At least one class of stock must be designated as voting common stock for this purpose. A prominent stockholder or one with a large number of shares may dominate the board of directors and be elected as both chairman of the board and chief executive officer. In 1985 it was estimated that 80 percent of corporations constituting the Fortune 500 companies had combination chairman/chief executive officer arrangements.[1]

A board may be composed of some combination of outside and inside directors. Inside directors hold administrative or staff responsibilities in the organization hierarchy, or in rare circumstances may be ordinary employees of the corporation. Outside directors are board members who have no employee affiliation with the organization. Outside members are usually selected because of their expertise (such as law), their name value (a prominent figure), or other possible contribution to the organization.

An advantage of inside directors is their intimate knowledge of the business and their ability to implement board policies directly. A disadvantage is the difficulty of exerting independence to represent stockholders while dependent on the president or board chairman for their continued employment. It may be risky to ask the hard questions that protect stockholder interests. Outside directors may lack the votes to challenge management when inside directors feel compelled to support management's positions.[2]

In 1985 alone, with the increases in litigation and increasing cost of director's liability insurance, the number of outside directors in the largest corporations declined from 63 percent to 57.5 percent of the board membership. Smaller organizations in general have fewer outside directors.

GOALS, STRATEGIES, AND PLANNING

The president, in a leadership role, develops organization objectives and goals, strategies for their attainment, policies to carry them out, and operating plans by which activities are structured and paid for. The board of directors' role is then to review and approve goals, strategies, and plans and assure that they are representative of stockholder interests in terms of risk, income, growth, and other objectives. Progress toward these ends is measured periodically and subjected to the oversight, evaluation, and control of the board of directors. Boards may convene routinely as often as monthly and as seldom as yearly. Between the meetings of the board, the president makes all operating decisions not reserved exclusively for the board. If business arises that must be deliberated by the full board, the president and the chairman of the board may schedule special meetings.

A special meeting of the board may be called at any time that a critical situation requires it. When it is difficult to schedule regular or special meetings at frequent intervals or on short notice, oversight and review may be delegated to committees of the board. Examples of committees may be the executive committee, an audit committee, a finance committee, committees for personnel, public relations, insurance, or other areas. In addition, ad hoc committees composed of selected people may be constituted to deal with a specific issue or problem.

THE BOARD OF DIRECTORS
AND OPERATING POLICIES

As a general rule, the board of directors should leave the officers of the organization free to run the business within established strategies and plans. There are day-to-day situations and problems that managers must deal with on a timely basis. Officers are generally selected on their ability to manage: to carry out operations as necessary, given an uncertain and changing environment, and to coordinate the complex activities that move an organization forward. But the board is ultimately responsible for management's actions. This responsibility may best be carried out on a continuous basis through participation in the establishment of the organization structure and its operating policies.

The Organization Structure

Most early concepts of organization structure have been based on principles of obtaining and using power, which were largely derived from early military and political systems. Modern organization theory has progressed a great deal since those early systems, but one finds the practical aspects of those systems still in place today. Thus it may be instructive to begin with the earlier concepts.

Absolute power in early political and military systems was held at the top of a system viewed as a pyramid. It was in turn delegated downward through layers of subordinates who were accountable to those under whom they served. Early accounting systems were reports to superiors on actions taken and funds used in carrying out their functions. Figure 8-1 illustrates and compares early military and political structures with their modern governmental and business organization equivalents.

In a more modern context, power can be defined as decision-making authority that is derived from one's position in the organization. A manager may choose to organize in such a way that authority is retained centrally and most important decisions are made by the manager. The complex environments

Figure 8-1
Traditional Formal Hierarchies of Power

MILITARY	MONARCHY	DEMOCRACY	BUSINESS
COMMANDER	KING	PRESIDENT	PRESIDENT
GENERALS	PRINCE	VICE PRESIDENT	VICE PRESIDENT
COLONELS	DUKE	DEPARTMENTS	DIVISIONS
CAPTAINS	EARL	BUREAUS	DEPARTMENTS
LIEUTENANTS	SQUIRE	OFFICES	SECTIONS

of most organizations make it difficult for one person to be effective in such a role.

Decision-making authority in organizations can be efficiently distributed through a decentralized organization structure. This permits a structure that recognizes the diversity of organization activities, yet provides an integration of them through various controls and information feedback mechanisms such as accounting, organization policies, and goal structures. Decentralization is often established under conditions of large organization size and/or high complexity of operations.

To be effective, decentralization requires that operations be subdivided by some logical differences in products, responsibilities, functions, or geographic areas that require specialized management education, experience, or expertise. The objective is to have divisions that can behave like independent organizations. It might be noted that one of the factors that created the move toward decentralization in large firms was the problem of obtaining relevant information on a timely basis. With the increasing availability of integrated computer networks, it may be possible for some previously decentralized decisions to be made centrally.

Directors must of course keep the interests of the organization as a whole uppermost in their frame of reference. Authority and responsibility may be delegated downward to decentralized division management, but coordination, oversight, and control should be retained in the central management function accountable to the board of directors. This process of dividing the organization into components and then integrating the components into the central purposes of the organization creates what might be called an inevitable conflict. That is, a decision made in the best interests of one division may not be in the best interests of the organization, or of other divisions. Management must consider carefully any intervention that might signal ambivalence regarding the amount of authority given to the division management, yet conflicts must be resolved. It may be necessary at times to allow a decentralized management view to prevail over a corporate-wide viewpoint in order to preserve divisional authority and autonomy and avoid a recentralization of decision making.

With the decentralization of management it has been noted that more complex relationships develop among divisions. Division managers begin to adopt some top management functions and behaviors, staff functions also tend to decentralize, financial affairs of investment and growth assume an increasing importance, and a larger volume of paperwork and communications networks develop. Independent divisions may engage in a costly competition with each other for sales. Dependent profit-center divisions that furnish goods and services to other divisions become concerned with transfer pricing—the prices charged to the buying division by the selling division, which must also make a profit on the exchange. Finally, central management people increasingly become concerned with adjudicating disputes among operating divisions and among staff departments.

At the board of directors level it may be noted that the central management officers, including the president, may be slower to respond to or be knowledgeable about questions concerning operations. The president may appear before the board surrounded by various staff and division officers in order to better field questions.

The responsibility for keeping the organization as a whole on track with its overall goals and strategies—control—becomes an important frame of reference for the directors. The stockholders' interests cannot be set adrift as directors find themselves submerged in operations problems. Increasingly, the budgeting process becomes the primary control instrument at the directors' level as at the president's level because it provides the overall resource allocation vehicle and the criteria against which performance can be measured and evaluated. The budget should be regarded as a contract in which management agrees to achieve specified outputs within the budgeted financial inputs.

An organization structure must of course provide a control climate—a process by which all activities are carried out according to plan or at least in a way that moves the organization toward its objectives and goals. The control climate involves choices among three methods or concepts of the elements of control.[3] These can be illustrated as follows:

CONTROL is a function of GOALS, PROCESSES, CONSTRAINTS

Goals can serve as a basis for control if they are seen as appropriate and worthwhile, are accepted by those involved, are well understood, and if creativity among organization participants is acceptable. Goal statements, company creeds, mottos, and codes of ethics can be used to reinforce this control concept.

Processes also serve as controls in the sense that prescribed routines and built-in checks are a part of the work design. If the work does not permit any deviations in the flow of activity, if there is a focus on one right way of doing things, if well-trained people are employed, and if internal checks are built into the system, the process may more or less control itself.

If goals cannot be well defined and accepted, and if the work cannot be tightly structured, control of a more direct type involving management constraints may be called for. That is, control is possible in unstructured environments through close supervision and instruction, demand for conformity to the rules of the workplace, employment of compliant personnel who accept direct supervision, and the ability to influence the behavior of subordinates through rewards and punishments.

Most organizations find it necessary to build their control systems around more than one of these concepts. If the controls correlate with organizational realities, the use of one or more of the above concepts can be successfully accomplished. Many organizations, Japanese firms in particular, have successfully used the goal basis of control. Organizations such as the Boy Scouts, engineering firms, and educational institutions can work well on such a basis.

Process control is also used successfully under the right conditions, and it, too, is indirect. That is, a good control through the design of work processes does not involve direct managerial interaction with workers to the extent that unstructured work does. A reliance on the constraint method of control is often required by the goals and requirements of the process. For example, prison administration might rely on combinations of process controls and constraints. Work involving unskilled labor may call for the use of constraints to the exclusion of goal- and process-related controls.

An organization that wishes to operate with a decentralized management function may have to give up much of its reliance on processes and constraints and attempt to establish a goal-centered philosophy to obtain control. The use of profit centers, investment centers, and cost centers with respect to organization structure reflects a goal-related division of effort. Accounting reports should be designed to conform to the structure and control philosophy of the organization.

Figure 8-2 illustrates a more comprehensive view of the sequential nature of a general control system. Goals establish the end results desired, while objectives represent specific attainments to be achieved. Out of goals and objectives, plans are formulated and resource outlays take place to carry out the work activity. Periodically, a measurement of results is made and subjected to a comparison in which that which actually occurred is compared with that which was planned. An evaluation of both plans and activities is thus possible. If corrective measures are called for, they can be instigated before it is too late to achieve the objectives.

A common error made in this process is to assume that the information about measured results is forwarded to higher-level managers. In order to be effective, it is important that the initial report of measured results and the comparison with plans be immediately available to the manager of the activity being measured. Thus, control through goals can be implemented. Only when corrective

Figure 8-2
Sequential Control Model

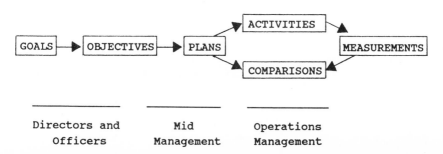

Figure 8-3
An Egalitarian View of the Organization Structure

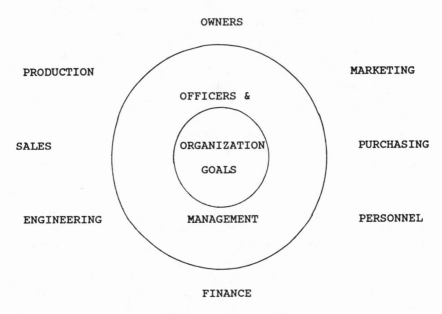

OWNERS

PRODUCTION   MARKETING

OFFICERS &

SALES   ORGANIZATION   PURCHASING

GOALS

ENGINEERING   MANAGEMENT   PERSONNEL

FINANCE

activity does not seem to be forthcoming at the level of the activity should a higher level of management become directly involved.

Some of the more recent concepts of organization are based on a more participative and perhaps egalitarian view that is founded on some of the concepts mentioned above: goals, information, achievement, systems, and managerial style and skills. In short, a goal-driven organization is the objective, rather than a power-driven structure. To some extent, goal-driven organizations may still show many aspects of the traditional pyramidal organization structure in order to seek a logical division of work, communication, and delegated responsibility. Figure 8-3 illustrates a less-structured organization design that emphasizes roles rather than rank and authority.

Accounting systems for both financial reporting and managerial reporting remain largely based on the formal pyramidal structure of the organization. Budgeting processes, too, tend to reflect the functional and activity grouping aspects of the organization in operation. Financial resources must eventually be used to support or produce a product or service for which someone or some department has administrative responsibility. Accounting is based on the association of cost with accomplishment. This can probably be done without regard to the way in which management chooses to operate, but it should reflect the organization structure if it is to be useful.

Operating Policies

A policy is a guide to future decisions, a frame of reference for a decision maker. An example is the policy that any purchase of materials exceeding $25,000 must be subject to competitive bidding procedures to assure the required quality at the lowest price and to avoid favoring certain vendors. Another example is the requirement that payments to individual employees that exceed a certain total amount must be approved by the personnel department. These examples might be referred to as controls. An administrative policy that managerial positions be filled from the ranks of present employees (promotion from within) would illustrate an operating policy rather than a control.

The board of directors should establish overall strategies and policies. They should also be apprised of and approve the policies of management and review them on a regular basis. It would be fair to ask, for example, "What would happen if the day's cash receipts were not deposited in the bank that same day?" Or "What happens when a manager resigns? How is the replacement selected?" The board itself can establish policies in areas of administrative concern or where an element of unavoidable operating risk exists. For example, the board may establish a policy that requires the "bonding" of employees with financial responsibilities or who have access to cash.

Some examples of policy areas that should be established by or considered by the board of directors are:

Policy	Area
financial structure	finance
selection of officers	personnel
organization structure	operations
banking arrangements	finance
issuance of debt or equity instruments	finance
operating budgets	finance
capital budgets	finance
international operations	operations
stockholder reports and meetings	legal
legal and ethical issues	legal
employee contracts, pay, and benefits	personnel
promotion practices	personnel
executive salaries and bonus arrangements	personnel
environmental concerns (waste and pollution)	legal
employment of minorities and disabled	personnel
insurance	finance
contracted professional services	operations

Policy	Area
audits	finance
product lines and pricing	operations
product manufacturing and distribution	operations
terms of sale and credit policies	operations
purchasing and contracting	operations
internal controls	operations

The existence of policies in guiding operating management allows the board to devote its attention to major problem areas that are not amenable to the establishing of policies. To illustrate the topics of most importance consider that among the top concerns of boards of directors in the Fortune 1000 companies in 1984 were:

- strategic planning
- top management performance and compensation
- planning for succession in management
- improving productivity
- monitoring corporate integrity[4]

BOARD STRUCTURE, AMBIENCE, AND "GOOD OLD BOY" NETWORKS

The corporate director should realize that financial information may be the basis for the oversight role, but that there are often obstacles to the successful access to, and use of, financial and other information. The most important and most subtle obstacle may be found in the environment of board decision making, which is further reviewed below and in Chapters 1 and 13.

The organization of a meeting of the board of directors must confront a dilemma. The board should function as a democracy, with full access to relevant information and the independence of each board member to vote as he or she sees fit. But at the same time, directors should know what to expect at a meeting and be provided the necessary data and viewpoints sufficiently in advance to allow the time to study and review reports and formulate questions. It is disruptive to have unexpected issues to resolve and insufficient background briefings to permit informed choices.

Hence, most board meetings follow an agenda—a structured series of reports to be given, approvals to be voted, and old and new issues needing attention. For example, the minutes must show the date, time, and place of the meeting, names of those in attendance, the nature of the meeting, and the presence of a quorum sufficient to conduct the business of the corporation. The bylaws of the quorum sufficient to conduct the business of the corporation. The bylaws of the corporation specify many of these requirements. Reports of the secretary, the treasurer, and the various permanent committees follow. Old business is reviewed to handle previous unresolved issues. New business is then taken up, but not "new" business in the sense of unplanned items. Ample notice of and information about new issues should be provided before the meeting. The meeting then adjourns. In the course of the meeting, strict adherence to a set of rules for conducting business, such as Robert's Rules of Order, will save much time and permit an orderly meeting to take place.

agenda may find it unpopular or even out of order to bring up really new business. He or she may find it necessary to approach the board chairman or most probably the president or CEO and attempt to bring up the issue in future meetings as an agenda item. It can be seen that the person or group that determines the agenda can have an inordinate amount of power over the deliberations of the board. Through the gatekeeping function, the president of the organization in effect controls the board of directors.

A former chairman of the Securities and Exchange Commission raised another important concern about the control of corporate directors. The meetings of the board are often held in a private-club atmosphere. Impressive surroundings, food and drink, and friendly conversation can be an overwhelming influence on the conduct of meetings. Depending on the nature of the business organization, directors' meetings are sometimes held in connection with sporting events, trade shows, or other interesting activities to provide an attraction to attend. Meetings may be held in various resort areas around the country. All of these promote a collegial ambience of good will and friendship that can quickly become a "good old boy" network or a "crony" system.[5]

One is not encouraged to challenge or openly question the viewpoints of others. Questions, challenges, or truly independent thought can be seen as a threat in such an environment. A director who disturbs the status quo may find it difficult to get his or her views expressed or to get items on the agenda. Real effectiveness as a director is then lost for all practical purposes.

How does a conscientious director deal with the high structuring of board meetings and the ambience that tends to lull the senses? A good deal of tact and diplomacy is required, but the focus on the oversight and controls responsibility should not be lost. One should not be Machiavellian, but concerns can be raised casually in seemingly idle conversations with officers and other board members. Issues can be phrased in a positive sense, such as "Could we be more helpful in this case if we looked into...", or "I like this move. Has anyone looked into..., however?" One may ask, "Do we have any legal advice on this?", or "I'm not clear on this. Could we hear from the controller to be sure we have the right picture?" The meeting itself is not the venue for real confrontation unless one is presented with an intractable problem and is willing to leave the board if it is not resolved.

If a good basis of support for one's position seems evident after an informal conversational polling of others, the director may talk to management or the chairman about studying the item and placing it on a future agenda. Such an approach to being an effective director may seem too indirect, manipulative, or ineffective to some, but a direct approach might not be effective at all if it involves confrontation with those who wield considerable power on the board. The Japanese emphasize a consensus approach to decision making that involves laying a foundation such as has been described above. An action or idea is circulated among various participants who can make suggestions and sign off on the issue. When a formal action is to be taken, there has already been a chance for behind-the-scenes inputs and most measures pass with little if any dissent at that time. Because of this approach, the Japanese Diet, or congress, passes a very high number of bills that come before it compared with a very low pass rate on bills in the U.S. Congress.

ASSERTING YOUR RIGHT TO KNOW

The board of directors has the right to any and all data available in the organization. Asserting that right can be difficult, however. Some information should be routinely available—notably financial information from the accounting and reporting system as discussed in earlier chapters. In addition, various operations reports and statistics should be routinely available. Such things as personnel turnover, legal actions, productivity, market strategies and position, new products and services, research in progress, and production and inventory status may be routine business of the board. If they are not, it is usually easy to get the cooperation of management in including such figures and others as regular reports to the board.

When a director finds that desired information "is not available," it may be necessary to raise questions. Common reasons given by officers are that "the computer is not programmed to do that," or that a government contract is involved and the data are classified. Other reasons are the sensitivity of the data because of a legal action, secrecy because of the competition, or the high cost of compiling the report. One may just have to accept some of these reasons or rethink the value and importance of the data wanted. Many questions or problems are suggested by the accounting, auditing, and budget reports, and this is often a legitimate basis for the director to seek further information. In general, board members may find more information available than they can handle.

The best strategy to gain information may be to seek general rather than specific responses, to draw attention to areas of concern rather than to challenge others, to offer praise for accomplishments rather than always being concerned with poor performance. When a real concern arises, the director can be more influential from a position of a good relationship with other directors and with corporate officers. A board member need not be overly timid or aggressive in pursuing the resolution of a perceived problem or issue. Management reports and other representations are usually presumed to be truthful unless a careful reading of available information does not bear out the facts given and assertions made. If the honesty of corporate officers becomes suspect, consideration should be given to conducting a special audit or to removal of the officer. This should be a rare occurrence indeed on most boards.

If the director is concerned about personal liability, it may be reassuring to know that courts have generally been sympathetic to the director's responsibility. The "business judgment" rule confers broad protection on directors when they follow rules of common sense. This means keeping informed, attending meetings, asking questions, developing some understanding of business affairs, assuring the presence of adequate accounting and administrative controls, and demonstrating some independence in board deliberations. The concept of business judgment has been well stated by the American Bar Association as follows:

A director who acts in good faith and in a manner he reasonably believes to be in the best interests of the corporation, who properly relies on information, opinions, reports and statements of others, who properly delegates certain functions traditionally associated with board activities, and who exercises free and independent business judgment, should find that state law imposes on him no further accountability.[6]

WHO RUNS THE BUSINESS?

A business is run at many levels. The work of producing goods and services occurs at the bottom of the pyramid illustrated in Figure 8-1. Department heads and supervisory people accomplish work through the direct efforts of people who do things. These may be unskilled, skilled, or professional people. They follow the plans (activities and schedules) set forth for them by higher levels of management. Large volumes of data are necessary at this level concerning inventories, personnel, suppliers, production, customers, and the inflow and outflow of resources.

At organizational units above the department, the business is run at the level called administration. Planning, coordinating, and integrating the work of various departments takes place here. This may be at the division level. The extensive data developed within operating departments are analyzed and summarized, and new data to aid the integrating and coordinating functions are introduced. Budgeting and budget reports comparing accomplishments with plans are produced. Controls that assure adherence to plans and policies are also administered at this level. Technological and competitive environments must also be assessed. Figure 8-2 illustrates some of these interactions, and the levels of management involvement are shown at the bottom of the figure.

Above the division level, operating and budgeting data are summarized even more and new information enters the system from both inside and outside the organization. Social, political, and economic changes in the organization's overall environment are monitored and interpreted. Various staff departments

Figure 8-4
Level, Volume, and Amount of Information

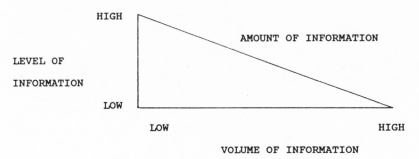

Source: Adapted from David H. Li, *Accounting Computers Management Information Systems* (New York: McGraw-Hill, 1968), p. 217.

may exist at this level to achieve the benefits of the expertise that can be provided by specialized knowledge people. In the terminology of management, staff functions are distinguished from line functions in that the latter are the people in the operating divisions and management who are directly involved in producing and selling the goods and services of the organization. It might be said that the business as a whole is run at the level of this interface of line and staff responsibilities.

What, then, of the board of directors? What does it "run"? Not much, really. It is not the board's function to conduct or supervise operations. Recall that in Chapter 1 the point was made that the board represents the stockholders in terms of providing review, approval, oversight, evaluation, and control of the organization's activities. The data requirements of the board tend to be highly summarized and largely are provided by those being evaluated and controlled: the top management.

Figure 8-4 places the various data requirements discussed above in perspective. At lower levels of information use, such as at the operations level, the required amount of information is high in volume and quite detailed. At successively higher levels of information use, information is summarized and reduced in volume. At the highest level of information use, such as the board level, the volume of information is greatly condensed. As an example, consider the return on investment figure. It relates the summary figure on the statement of income to the summary figure on the statement of financial position to produce a single measurement: profit in relation to total assets. As other data comprising these totals are added, the level of information is decreased and volume is increased.

Note that the figure shows that for every level of information use, the volume of information required to achieve the appropriate amount is different. The appropriate amount of information is a product of its volume and level. A phenomenon called information overload is produced when an excessive volume of information is made available at a given decision level. A list of delinquent customer accounts receivable would be inappropriate at the level of the board of directors, and perhaps even at the level of higher management, for example. On the other hand, the total dollar amount of delinquent receivables would be too summarized for effective use by the credits and collection department.

Each level of the hierarchy of an organization, following the model in Figure 8-4, should be provided with the appropriate level and volume of information. That is one of the primary responsibilities of the corporate controller in the design of accounting and reporting systems. Various levels within the organization structure must receive information relevant to operating decisions for its part of the whole, yet the information should be in a form that facilitates an aggregation of each part into a unified information structure.

CONCLUSION

To some, this may appear to be a strange chapter in a financial handbook for corporate directors. It may help to remember that financial data have as their purpose not only the reporting of information, but also its effective use for appropriate purposes.

Directors must often base interactions with officers on the underlying data system of financial information. Many policies are related to or affected by accounting and financial criteria. The way in which the board interacts with management must be understood if the director is to put the information available to effective use. Finally, it is important for the director to be able to ascertain the right amount and uses of information to avoid both too much information or too little.

NOTES

1. "Inside Look at Life in the Corporate Board Room," Interview with Robert K. Mueller, Chairman, Arthur D. Little, Inc., *U.S. News and World Report*, January 28, 1985, p. 72.

2. "The Job Nobody Wants," *Business Week*, September 8, 1986, p. 57.

3. John P. Fertakis, "Toward a Theory of Control in Organizations," *Western Tax Review* 6, No. 2 (Fall 1985), pp. 168–181.

4. Survey of Board Chairmen of Fortune 1000 companies, Heidrich and Struggles, reported in *The Week in Review*, Deloitte Haskins & Sells, 84-12, 1984.

5. These views are also briefly explored in "The Job Nobody Wants," pp. 60–61.

6. American Bar Association, *Corporate Director's Guidebook* (Chicago, 1978), p. 21. (Reprinted from *The Business Lawyer* 33, No. 3 [April 1978]. © 1978 by the American Bar Association.)

CHAPTER 9

THE DIRECTOR AND COMPANY OPERATIONS

The major recurring areas of management concern in organizations lie in what are called operations. Operations consist of the ongoing day-to-day activities that bring in revenues from customers or clients. The Statement of Income prepared by accountants highlights captions such as "operating income" or "income from operations" or "income from continuing operations," as distinct from "net" income, which includes nonoperating factors that influence the status of stockholders. If a firm is to become successful, it must do well in operations.

In the narrow sense of the term, operations refers to manufacturing activities of organizations. The managers in these areas are typically people with scientific and engineering expertise. Technical problem-solving ability is highly valued. In the traditional management literature, scientific management was concerned with the one best way to do manufacturing tasks. People were but another engineering element to be integrated with machinery and work flows in the plant. The U.S. reputation for quality products and organization efficiency was built on these concepts.

In more recent times, the application of scientific principles and concepts to business operations grew to include not only science and engineering but also psychology, sociology, anthropology, mathematics, and other sciences. Important concepts and models were developed in such areas as production scheduling, machine utilization, process design, inventory control, cost engineering, the effect of learning on cost behavior, deriving optimum production order quantities and order frequency, statistical quality control, cybernetics, systems theory, decision theory, and many other areas based on a wider range of human knowledge and experience. The term *scientific management* was reversed, in effect, and became known as *management science*.

The broad applicability of these concepts and methods expanded the meaning of operations. Operations in the broader perspective of today include all functions that are now considered line responsibilities: those that have decision-making authority in the functional performance areas of the business. These include production, marketing, administration, finance, and many related functional specialties.[1]

Operating decisions are generally the responsibility of the officers and managers selected to lead the organization. The board of directors is not likely to have strong participation in such decisions, though the review and oversight responsibility looms large in this area. A typical board will delegate its operations responsibility to an executive or operations subcommittee of the board. The audit committee, too, may find itself considering operating problems and control problems brought out in the report of the independent auditor.

A 1987 report on the types of questions asked at annual meetings of the corporation indicates a considerable interest in operations on the part of shareholders.[2] Not only that, but there exists a greater depth of knowledge and understanding than one might think there is in the shareholder group. Such questions are normally posed to the organization's operating officers, but the director should be knowledgeable about this area and interested in the answers given or avoided by officers.

BASIC OPERATIONS FUNCTIONS

All firms must identify or select an area of service or product need that they can effectively serve in terms of profitability. They must recruit, hire, and train managers, staff, and support personnel, as well as those who are responsible for performing a professional service or for producing goods and related services. Organizations must provide the space and equipment needed to carry on business and provide levels of inventories adequate to support sales. They must identify potential customers and advertise the organization's product or service. They must establish appropriate prices and terms of sale and delivery, and collect amounts due on a timely schedule. Finally, organizations must pay creditors and employees as required and manage funds in a competent manner. Operations thus consist of a wide variety of efforts that must be coordinated and directed toward the organization's goals.

MEASURING PERFORMANCE

As with the company as a whole, the performance of divisions and/or managers is usually measured in financial terms as well as physical measurements. Accounting measurement, for example, may focus on the control of costs within an operation that is constituted as an organization function or department. The cost center thus is measured and evaluated on its ability to stay within planned costs or to achieve cost reductions while achieving its planned output of goods and services. Another accounting measurement basis is the profitability of the department or function: the profit center approach. This basis for measuring performance allows the manager of the operation to balance both costs and revenues, without close monitoring of either by superiors as long as planned levels of profits are achieved.

The investment center basis for measuring performance achieves the widest delegation of responsibility to operations managers. The primary performance measurement is the profitability of the unit in comparison with the capital investment utilized. The unit is thus evaluated as though it were an independent business. The manager's responsibility is to control costs, maximize revenues, and also to invest in productive assets that can be effectively utilized in producing products and services and provide an adequate return on the resources invested. A division of the business that competes in the electronics industry can be evaluated by management in comparison with independent electronics firms' financial performance in the total economy.

Other operations performance measurements include productivity measurements, product quality measurements, share of the market measurements, rate of growth during the period, cash flow produced, and others. Ultimately, however, success in these other dimensions should be reflected in superior financial performance that is measured in financial measurements and general-purpose accounting statements.

The most widely used overall standard for the measurement of achievement is the comparison of financial results against the budget. A discussion of basic budgeting concepts was presented in Chapter 6. The budget serves as a control over operations in that it sets forth cost, profit, and return-on-investment goals that motivate and guide operations managers in balancing the relevant performance factors.

Managing through the participative establishing of budgeted or operational goals between superiors and subordinates is referred to variously as results management, management by exception, or management by objectives. While objectives can be imposed on subordinates unilaterally by superiors, there are many benefits that arise from soliciting participation, such as better communication and understanding, better motivation, and improved personal relationships between levels of management. Imposed goals can be effective in the short run, but can be troublesome in the long run as increasingly higher goals are perceived by subordinates as being exploitative. Either imposed or participative goal-setting processes and the natural movement toward improved performance and tougher goals can result in increasing pressure being felt by operations people.

THE SPECIALIZATION OF MANAGEMENT

In carrying out operations, organizations often tend to seek personnel with specialized expertise and knowledge in each area of effort. An important management function then becomes that of integrating and coordinating various specialized activities and departments into a coherent whole. Staff specialties usually arise in areas of operations such as personnel, training, product development, procurement, production, scheduling, wage and salary administration, finance, marketing, and advertising.

As layers of expertise and specialization become interposed between managers at the top and workers at the bottom of the organization hierarchy, a peculiar phenomenon arises: Advice from operations specialists and staff personnel tends to become authoritative. That is, as management receives advice and recommendations for decisions from highly specialized experts, often with a language of their own, it becomes risky to ignore this advice, or to ask questions that may reveal an inability to understand the recommendations made. The final operations decisions then tend to become, in effect, the decisions of the experts. Moving on the recommendations of staff and specialists is a safe course for the manager since a bad decision, made contrary to staff recommendations, is likely to be a setback to the manager's career. On the other hand, a bad decision, following recommendations made by highly paid experts, gives the manager a somewhat safer position. An experienced administrator should keep staff advice in perspective and sometimes go with his or her own intuition in spite of the risks associated with this action.

A greater reliance on staff and operations specialists also has the effect of distancing higher-level managers from everyday operations. Even well-established production technology is sometimes difficult to grasp in the sense of exercising close supervision and management. Controls often center on setting objectives with operating management and relying on their competence and motivation to achieve the targeted results. Management by exception and management by objectives represent control philosophies that depend on the competence and professionalism of operations managers rather than a detailed understanding of the operations themselves by higher levels of management.

As operations involve increasingly complex high technology products, services, or manufacturing processes, and increasingly ambiguous markets and competitive environments, higher management people must of necessity move away from the work itself and become managers of people and organization structures. How, then, can the review, oversight, and control functions of the board be exercised in the operations of the firm? This is considered in the last section of this chapter.

MANAGEMENT FRAUD

Another potential operations problem arises in the pressure on subordinates to achieve success in meeting high performance expectations. When operations managers are subject to objectives and budgets that are difficult to achieve, they may tend to cheat on performance measurements or challenge either the objectives or the process of measuring performance. The SEC has become increasingly concerned about the extent of financial manipulation of production and sales figures caused by internal pressures, and the related effects on financial reports.[3]

Inaccurate financial reporting has generally been attributed either to errors and systems deficiencies, or to fraud and theft. Public auditing procedures have primarily focused on the former. While there was some importance attached to the discovery of fraud and theft, it was felt in the profession that such activities would be uncovered in the course of examining the underlying operating and accounting systems for errors and system problems. The audit was typically not designed specifically to look for fraud and theft unless there was evidence or suspicion from other sources that such had occurred. New auditing objectives have recently been considered by national accounting and auditing groups in response to those who view this approach as inadequate.

The new element of concern about the accuracy and reliability of financial reports stems from the actions of people in the context of results management and management by objectives. The management philosophy of setting goals with the participation of subordinates and allowing managers freedom in meeting them is often accompanied by loose internal controls. Without tough internal controls, mid-level managers may be encouraged to play with the numbers that eventually reach financial reports. The intentional manipulation of operations and financial information for the purpose of measuring up to a superior's expectations rather than for personal gain is not specifically contemplated in the design of auditing procedures.

The SEC investigated a number of "book-cooking" cases and found that substantially all such cases had the common elements of:

- a distant central management authority,
- considerable pressure to meet goals,
- lack of accountability for methods used to achieve goals, and
- weak internal controls to assure compliance with operating policies.

In all cases, the books were altered to paint a better picture of performance, not to conceal fraud or theft or diversion of assets.[4]

REVIEW, OVERSIGHT, AND CONTROL

The board of directors and its audit committee might well inquire about whether schedules and goals set for departments are realistic and reasonable, whether adequate resources are made available, whether strong behavioral guidelines and policies are in place, and whether effective internal controls are built into operating systems and reporting procedures. One may view the procession that leads from goal setting to evaluation in four segments that identify the pressures and responses commonly involved:

1. *Organization Goals and Personal Goals.* The operating objectives established for the manager are fixed in a framework of individual goals such as success, promotion, wealth, prestige, and others. Pressure exists to succeed in all areas.

2. *Performance.* High expected levels of achievement increase the possibility of failure, thus jeopardizing personal goal attainment. Pressure thus increases. One may recall the line, "I don't care how you get it done, but get it done."

3. *Measurement of Performance.* As performance falls behind, mistakes are made, or inappropriate actions occur, and pressure rises to create the illusion of performance by falsifying measurements or attacking the validity of the measurement system.

4. *Evaluation.* A natural pressure arises to focus activities on those aspects of performance that produce rewards, while suboptimizing or neglecting other aspects of performance. The goal may thus be achieved and a favorable evaluation received while leaving the wreckage of operations behind: poor morale, neglected maintenance, wasted parts, dissatisfied customers, and possible illegal actions.

Fraud in organizations is usually likely where structural pressures are high, the number of possible opportunities for fraud are high, and where the integrity and personal characteristics of the individual are low. The design and operation of accounting and other internal control systems already discussed can serve to minimize the opportunity factor.

The extent of organizational pressures can be assessed by managers and directors (who may be the source of such pressures in the first place). Pressure can be justified if performance is well below an expected and reasonable level of efficiency. It can also serve well in a crisis such as meeting a deadline, or solving an operational problem. People can feel a sense of pride and accomplishment when such problems are corrected and a period of normal operations with reduced pressure follows. But pressure for high achievement should not be an ongoing, systematic, psychological pressure to meet difficult long-term goals or to accomplish objectives with inadequate resources of personnel and facilities.

The third factor above, integrity and personal characteristics, should be addressed in all personnel selection and promotion decisions. The firm should employ persons of ability and good character and attempt to communicate to them a sense of values. A corporate culture that honors hard work, honesty, and a cooperative spirit should be promoted. The highest value should be service to those who buy the company's products and services.

A code of ethics governing managerial behavior should also be developed and strongly supported by officers and directors. Ethics is not merely obeying the law, but also means doing the right thing. Lying about performance, taking credit for the work of others, and giving expensive presents to obtain favorable consideration are not illegal actions, but they are certainly unethical. If this type of activity is condoned or overlooked, it can spread to others and eventually harm the organization. Corporate codes should go beyond conflicts of interest and infractions against the corporation itself. They should also stress the firm's role in civic and social matters and at least pay some attention to consumer relations, environmental safety, and product quality.

OPERATING CYCLES:
ANOTHER VIEW

An approach to understanding operations that may be instructive for the director is that of an auditing point of view. Auditors are not managers, and do not have an in-depth understanding of specific corporate operations, yet must be able to develop an overview for purposes of examining the workings of the operating systems.

One may think of operations in terms of operating cycles that the organization should do well if it is to succeed. The cycles can be approached independently of the operations specialties discussed earlier in this chapter because the income report adequately reveals how well things are operating as a whole. The review of cycles of operations that lead to profitability can be made at the bottom of the decision hierarchy rather than the top or middle.

The accounting firm of Arthur Andersen & Co. has attempted to reduce the economic events and the resulting "web of transactions, systems, processing procedures, interfaces, and data bases" into a limited and simplified number of groups or activities. The adequacy of internal controls and the effectiveness of each activity can then be evaluated. Figure 9-1 presents the Arthur Andersen approach. Not only transactions, but physical control of various assets can be linked to the cycles shown in Figure 9-1. Cash and securities, for example, are controlled by the treasury cycle. Inventories and property are the responsibility of the conversion cycle (which may involve either manufacturing or service types of activities).

Financial reporting is the fifth cycle in the Arthur Andersen approach, but no transactions are processed here. The goal of this fifth cycle is timely reporting of relevant data to the people and groups that must rely on such data in the performance of their responsibilities. This includes managers, officers and directors, stockholders, creditors, and others.

Each cycle in turn consists of various functions that can be observed and evaluated. For example, the expenditure cycle includes the acquisition of, and payment for

Figure 9-1
Common Activity Cycles in Organizations

ECONOMIC EVENTS THAT ARE CONVERTED INTO TRANSACTIONS	CYCLES OF ACTIVITY
1. Capital funds are received from investors and creditors	
	TREASURY
2. Capital funds are temporarily invested until needed for operations	
3. Resources (goods and services) are acquired from vendors and employees in exchange for obligations to pay	EXPENDITURE
4. Obligations to vendors and employees are paid	
5. Resources are held, used, or transferred	CONVERSION
6. Resources are distributed to outsiders in exchange for promises of future payments	
	REVENUE
7. Outsiders pay for resources distributed to them	

Source: Adapted from *A Guide for Studying and Evaluating Internal Accounting Controls.* (Chicago: Arthur Andersen & Co., 1978), p. 14.

- Property, plant, and equipment;
  Goods (inventories) used directly in the production process or in the furnishing of services or acquired for resale;
- Personal services, i.e. payroll, whether direct labor, indirect labor, executive and administrative, functional, etc.;
- Supplies, whether used in production or otherwise; and
- Outside services, such as electricity, water, telephone and telegraph, legal and accounting, marketing research, etc....
- Taxes, rents, and royalties.[5]

The expenditure cycle may be represented by organizational departments such as Purchasing, Payroll, Receiving, and Contracting. Of course there are overlapping elements of each cycle and function (interfaces) since each must interact and coordinate with others. Other cycles can similarly be broken down into a number of functions performed by departments or divisions within the organization.

The term *operations*, in this view, consists of the day-to-day activities and transactions of the treasury, expenditure, conversion, and revenue cycles. A detailed examination of the concept of cycles of activity is beyond the scope of this book. Suffice it to say that if one views the operations of business organizations in terms of the primary activities that take place and the way they interrelate, the apparent complexity of business can be reduced.

CURRENT DEVELOPMENTS

The increasing competition of foreign manufacturers and service organizations has been alarming. U.S. firms have been criticized for their complacency and the poor product quality, wasteful practices, and operating inefficiences that result. The loss of market share in traditionally strong industries and the decrease in profitability caused by price competition and high production costs are stimulating a rethinking of operating practices in many companies. The improvement of product and service quality and the restructuring of costs have received increasing attention by management.

A majority of the improved practices being considered by operations management are found in Japanese firms. Many of these practices are based on concepts originating in the United States, but rejected by management in favor of a comfortable status quo. Concepts and practices in areas such as product quality improvement, inventory control, product design, robotics, and employee involvement have been restudied and newly adopted in some firms in the United States. A detailed discussion of these concepts and practices is beyond the scope of this book, but two ideas are briefly reviewed below as examples.

Quality Control

Product quality has often been viewed in the past as a management and engineering responsibility. If the machinery can be made more reliable and if output is inspected to reduce the number of unsatisfactory items shipped, it was felt that good overall quality could be achieved. The Japanese operate on the principle that quality is everyone's job. Each worker is responsible for the inspection of his or her own work and the correction of quality problems before the product goes to the next operation or to the customer. Through worker groups called quality circles, employees are encouraged to suggest changes that would improve the reliability of each operation and the quality of the firm's products. If problems of quality appear, the work of the department can be stopped until the problem is corrected. Recognition and awards are given to workers who suggest quality improvement and/or lower-cost practices. The costs of quality control and inspections should thus be greatly reduced.

The commitment to total quality is also passed on to suppliers. Instead of having to inspect deliveries and negotiate problems with vendors, the firm requires vendors to deliver defect-free materials. Vendors who cannot guarantee the expected quality of goods on schedule are listed as less preferable sources and sometimes excluded from further dealings. If this concept is satisfactorily implemented, the account for "Purchases Returns and Allowances" should be drastically reduced. Other costs such as inspectors, paperwork for returning and reordering goods, and rework and waste should also be reduced.

Inventory Control

The purpose of inventories in most firms is to decouple purchasing and manufacturing operations from sales operations. The inventory buffers or absorbs the differences in the production operations, which desire long production runs and a steady state environment, and the sales operations, which strive for flexibility to meet variations in demand in whatever pattern they develop. Consequently, the inventory investment is considerable at times. There are inventories of purchased materials awaiting use in production, floor inventories between work stations, and inventories of finished goods awaiting sale. Of course this pattern requires storage space for materials and finished goods, and more space between work stations for partially finished pieces awaiting the next operation. In all probability, forklift machinery and conveyors are needed to move items along. A need for a larger building and more land for storage is often the result. The amount of investment capital tied up in inventories, space, and other costs can be considerable.

The Japanese have adopted a technique called "just-in-time" (JIT) inventory management to overcome some of the above problems. In essence, this practice recouples purchasing, manufacturing, and sales operations. Materials arrive "just in time" to be used in manufacturing, and goods are manufactured "just in time" for delivery to sales outlets or customers. This system is often implemented as a "pull" inventory system in contrast to the "push" system described in the previous paragraph. The ultimate condition in JIT is an inventory of one unit or batch of goods at each stage of manufacture. When a sale of one unit or batch is made, it pulls a similar quantity through manufacturing, and this in turn pulls materials from suppliers to replace the quantity used in production. Of course this is the ideal and is not likely to be achieved, but there is some quantity less than that previously on hand that can be achieved in most cases.

The JIT system requires a capability to respond quickly to variations in sales volumes. Obstacles have been the set-up time and cost ordinarily required to recalibrate machinery and change the configuration of the process for each of several products that may share the same operations. The set-up costs have been a major engineering challenge because they typically stop production for periods as long as several hours or even days. This, too, has been a focus of Japanese production methods. A goal here is an automatic or one-step changeover capability that creates a minimum set-up period or interruption in the operation.

As inventories are reduced, smaller facilities become practical. Work stations can be closer together, inventory waste reduced, conveyors eliminated, and investment dollars and interest pared significantly. Production problems and supply problems become quickly evident in JIT systems, but are viewed as a challenge for engineers and managers to overcome inefficiency and organizational problems revealed by a more responsive system.

Other concepts and practices credited to the Japanese are under study, such as life-time employment, consensus management, and employee motivation, reward, and promotion systems. It should be realized, though, that the reasons many of these techniques are successful in Japan are its short distances and industrial concentration, the long cultural history of Japan, the attitudes and education of its people, its national identity and cohesiveness, and its less aggressive labor union movement. Whether these practices based on Japan's environment can be transferred successfully to the United States remains to be seen. Enough progress has been made in some areas, notably quality control and inventory management, that there is hope that these ideas and practices will take root in the United States. Japanese firms locating in the United States have been able to implement many of the practices in the U.S. environment that have been successful in Japan.

CONCLUSIONS

The director cannot, and probably should not, provide review, oversight, and control of detailed operations functions. The board of directors should, however, be alert to elements of financial reports that may indicate inefficiency, problems, or failures in the underlying cycles and functions. An unusual decrease or increase in sales revenue, increase in cost of goods sold, or a significant change in reported inventories, sales, purchase returns, interest costs, or other categories might suggest a tactful question to management.

Audit reports, too, may contain information on areas of activity that are deficient, lacking control, or that need improvements in operating procedures. The auditing committee of the board of directors should receive the full audit report given to management, including accompanying letters and exhibits. The committee should also question auditors and seek further information about areas of concern. The full board should be apprised of all areas of operations for which a problem or concern was raised by the auditors.

The board member should realize that the operations of the firm are placed under the responsibility of duly selected officers and managers. The decisions as to what to do, how to do it, and whether to do it are in the hands of the organization hierarchy. An "activist" board member seeking a more direct involvement with operations decisions may find him- or herself relegated to the sidelines with diminished influence over corporate affairs. But more on this in Chapter 13.

NOTES

1. An early work that defined the new dimensions and techniques of operations is David W. Miller and Martin K. Starr, *Executive Decisions and Operations Research* (Englewood Cliffs, N.J.: Prentice-Hall, 1960).

2. *Shareholder Questions* (New York: Price Waterhouse, 1987).

3. John M. Fedders and L. Glenn Perry, "Policing Financial Disclosure Fraud: The SEC's Top Priority," *The Journal of Accountancy*, July 1984, pp. 58–64.

4. Adapted from a speech by SEC commissioner James C. Treadway, Jr., reported in *Accounting Events and Trends* (New York: Price Waterhouse, June–July, 1983).

5. Excerpted, with permission, from *A Guide for Studying and Evaluating Internal Accounting Controls.* (Chicago: Arthur Andersen & Co., 1978), pp. 21–22.

CHAPTER 10

ELEMENTS OF
COST CONTROL:
A DIRECTOR'S VIEW

Profit is the result of two elements measured in accounting terms: revenues and costs. Profits can be increased by initiating some activity that produces revenue in excess of the cost of that activity. Profits can also be increased by controlling the costs of existing activities. The activities that can be initiated to increase revenues are many and varied. They generally involve forecasting, planning, innovating, and decision making. As proposals come before the board of directors, there are few guarantees of success and various degrees of risk that must be evaluated. Decisions usually involve changing markets, changing prices, introducing new products or services, or developing new competitive strategies.

Similarly, controlling costs should be viewed as equally complex and challenging. Cost control also involves forecasting, planning, innovating, and decision making. Success is not guaranteed, and there are degrees of risk that must be considered. Organizations often view cost control in overly simple terms, however. Attempts to control costs should not impair revenues or hamper innovations, nor should they produce other costs that negate the savings produced by the actions taken. To give an extreme example, management can reduce labor costs by decreasing the size of work crews, but as production falls behind and workers feel exploited by the pressure to perform, there are further revenue and cost impacts that can affect profits adversely. As the director listens to management's proposed responses to revenue and cost problems, a better grasp of the oversight responsibility can be attained by considering the more specific nature of cost control that is discussed in this chapter.

THE COST PROBLEM

"How much will it cost?" "How can we bring our costs under control?" At some point in almost every business decision, these questions arise.[1] The essence of these questions is that a decision is at hand or a problem exists and the level of projected or actual cost is an important concern.

The first question indicates a concern that the planned course of action may be too costly to undertake. Costs should be as low as possible, not only to make the plan feasible, but also to improve the expected profitability as much as possible. The second question implies that costs are higher than planned and that steps should be taken to reduce whatever factors are contributing to the problem. It is hardly surprising then that cost control becomes associated with cost minimization. But these are only two dimensions of what is meant by cost control—and there are other dimensions as well. This chapter reviews management's concern with costs and explores and explains the more specific meanings of cost control in management.

MANAGING COSTS

A plan to do something becomes real only with the outlay of cost factors such as money, time, effort, and other sacrifices. In business and government, cost factors are measured in terms of money or its equivalent—making them readily comparable with revenues and other benefits, also measured in money terms. When projected or actual costs are high relative to benefits, costs and their control become important concerns of management. Figure 10-1 illustrates the framework within which the level of costs is an important consideration. The figure illustrates two levels of management concern. First, activities should be consistent with plans if goals are to be achieved. Second, benefits should exceed costs if efforts are to be successful in an economic sense.

Figure 10-1
Planning and Using Resources in Business

The control of costs is important to the success of the enterprise and its participants. The view that cost control is synonymous with cost reduction is an impediment to management's real understanding of the scope of actions available to them. Four dimensions of cost control can be readily identified, and each is important as a distinct management tool: cost engineering, cost control, cost reduction, and cost optimization. Each dimension is unique in its application by management and in the results achievable in planning and controlling operations.

Cost Engineering

Cost engineering is the design of products, methods, processes, and organization for a desired balance between cost and other factors. In planning, it is important to establish the relative weight to be given to a product's form and function, quality and reliability, and cost. In most cases all of these factors must be considered and incorporated in the final decisions. However, choices must sometimes be made between high quality and low cost, for example. The final product design may evolve to a reasonable quality of the product with a cost appropriate to that objective. Figure 10-2 illustrates the trade-offs involved in cost engineering.

Figure 10-2
Cost Engineering Factors

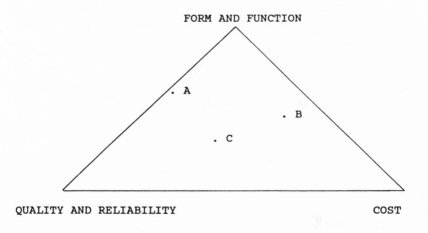

Source: Modified from Donald R. Herzog, "Research in New Product Planning," *Marketing Insights*, January 20, 1969, pp. 8–9.

The point identified as "A" in Figure 10-2 might illustrate the relative weighting of factors in designing and producing an experimental shale oil refinery, a recoverable space vehicle, or a medical instrument cathode ray tube. Where an element of emergency or danger might accompany the use of the product, development and production costs may be relatively insignificant criteria for decisions. Point "B" might be more appropriate to a standard production-run automobile or a home video recorder. The product must be priced in a competitive market, and low cost is one of the primary considerations in the product design in order to achieve profitability. Point "C" could illustrate considerations given to the design of a photographic slide changer within a projector, or an automobile radiator. It is important to assure the reliable operation of the component and a cost that assures a profitable sale of the product itself. The form of the product is relatively unimportant since it is out of sight and must only fit within the space allotted to that function within the machine.

Cost engineering is dependent on identifying the user of the product, the needs of the user, the appropriate market and pricing strategy, and the resources and technology to be employed. Once plans take shape and resources are committed, cost becomes relatively structured within the production process and cost planning is replaced by cost control.

Cost Control

The focus of cost control is the maintenance of costs at their planned level. Without monitoring, activities often tend to incur costs that are at variance with plans. At one extreme is the rapid rise in costs due to inefficiency and waste in the production organization and its management. On the other hand, an unplanned reduction in costs may signal a slippage in the quality of the product, shortcuts being taken in the production process, or materials of cheaper quality being purchased for use in production.

The emphasis of cost control is to adhere to prescribed levels of product quality, resource use, and methods of work. Typical cost control efforts take the form of: assignment of responsibility, establishing and communicating standards, measuring and communicating results, and executive action and follow-up. Achieving cost control must itself be effective and accomplished at a reasonable cost. A typical control is the measurement and reporting of cost variances (cost higher or lower than planned) by the cost accounting department. These are incorporated as part of the basic accounting measurement system through standard costing or budgetary analysis. Reports that highlight significant variations from the standard or budget can motivate those managers responsible for performance to themselves analyze and correct the causes of unplanned costs.

The application of cost control can often be efficiently directed to areas of most importance by considering the relationships observed long ago by Vilfredo

Pareto.[2] While Pareto was observing the pattern of income distribution in society, his "curve" has many modern applications. Expressed in a broader context, it can be noted that in any population of people or things, about 10 to 20 percent of the population accounts for 80 to 90 percent of various measured characteristics of the population. This relationship can be observed, for example, in the number of people having the highest income and the percentage of the total population income they represent. We might also observe, to continue the example, that the 20 percent of the people having the highest personal income account for 80 percent of all income earned in the population as a whole. Similar relationships may be found in:

- the parts that fail most frequently in a product, and the total number of parts;
- the people involved in the most accidents, and all people having accidents;
- the highest cost items in the inventory, and the dollars invested in inventory;
- the production operations with the highest costs, and the cost of all operations performed;
- the people filing the most grievances, and the total number of grievances filed;
- the highest-priced items sold, and the total sales revenue generated.

Expenditures for cost control should be directed primarily to those few operations, items, or departments that account for the highest proportion of total cost. Good cost control in significant cost-incurring areas can be obtained relatively inexpensively by a selective rather than across-the-board application of controls. For example, critical high-cost inventory items—perhaps 20 percent of the items accounting for 80 percent of the inventory investment—can be ordered using an "economic order quantity" formula. This method carefully controls each "A" item to minimize the amount carried, while also minimizing the chances of running out before the new stock arrives.

The lowest-cost items, composing perhaps 50 percent of the inventory and 10 percent of the inventory investment, might be classified as "C" items and ordered twice a year in six-month quantities. In a sense, control of these items can yield little cost improvement so little effort is expended. The remaining 30 percent of items carried ("B" items) may be placed on a "two bin" system in which an order is placed each time one of the two bins carrying each item is emptied. Adequate control at low cost is thus assured. Such an "ABC" inventory system can reduce inventory carrying value and assure parts availability. Tight control is assured over critical items and looser control is allowed over others, using selective and cost effective control tools. Carrying this example one step further, differential purchasing policies can help control costs. "A" items might be purchased on the basis of competitive bidding; "B" items on fixed longer-term contracts, and "C" items at prevailing market prices.

Other cost controls can be achieved by various means such as better recruitment, selection, and retention of skilled people; employee training; ensuring that equipment is adequately serviced and repaired; promoting good communication of plans and standards throughout the organization; and compliance-oriented supervisory practices.

The importance of executive action on cost problems and subsequent follow-up on results achieved cannot be too strongly emphasized. If cost control is perceived as important in the organization and in the work environment, and if persistent variances elicit management concern and possible sanctions, many cost problems will be handled at levels of management closest to areas of performance, consistent with principles of management decentralization and management by objectives. If costs are judged to be excessive, a program of cost reduction may be in order.

Cost Reduction

Cost reduction refers to processes used to bring costs to a level lower than the present or expected level, without impairing future company profits or its survival.[3] The question becomes whether the output the company has decided to produce can be produced more inexpensively or whether resources could be combined in such a way as to lower the total resources required. Is there waste that can be avoided that is greater than the cost of avoiding it? When the prices of resources change, it is appropriate to consider whether the combination of resources can be changed to prevent a rise or bring about a reduction in the cost of production.[4]

A primary method to reduce costs is to redesign the product or its method of production—or in the case of a service, to redefine its scope and process and delivery. New materials or methods may have become available, parts may have been overdesigned for the function they perform. A switch that may last 50 years may be inappropriate for an electric lawnmower typically used for only ten years or so. Again, Pareto's relationships may help identify high-cost parts or operations toward which cost reduction efforts can be directed with the highest potential benefit. Of perhaps 150 parts, 15 may account for 90 percent of the total parts costs incurred for a given product. Added employee training or improved personnel practices to reduce employee turnover costs, refinancing organizational debt, subcontracting parts of the work, or contracting out unused capacity are just a few areas of good potential cost reduction.

Hunt identifies several levels of cost reduction effort, ranging from "spring house cleaning" (eliminate frills, lax supervision, lazy or incompetent workers, etc.), to "crisis management" of operating losses or cash shortages (meat axe cuts of operations, across-the-board reductions, etc.), to "planned reductions" (cost reduction committees, special cost or operations analyses, operations or management audits, etc.).[5]

Cost reduction efforts may be short-term or long-term in nature, though they often arise from longer-term considerations. They often deal with possible strategic impacts on the company and its products or services. Work standards, evolving labor perquisites, product quality, and many other factors in the life of an organization are potentially affected by cost reduction actions.

Cost reduction efforts may be expected to achieve important benefits to the organization, but expectations should be kept to a reasonable level. In a *Wall Street Journal* article, Wickham Skinner warns that cost reduction efforts may not produce the competitive benefits often expected.[6] The pressure to reduce costs beyond a reasonable point can cause undesirable effects in the work force. The answer seems to lie more than ever before in improving product quality, delivery, service, and reliability. Reducing the time required to take an idea from a plan to the actual production and delivery of products and services has become an important competitive requirement in world markets. There may be an opportunity for a net cost reduction as the time involved in product decisions diminishes. An overall study, analysis, and restructuring of costs may be called for to meet longer-term strategic cost and competitive problems.

Cost Optimization

Sometimes called cost-effectiveness analysis, cost optimization refers to efforts to (1) achieve a given benefit at the lowest cost, or (2) achieve the most benefit for a given level of cost. In this dimension of cost control, the identification of benefits desired is a most important point of departure. Business revenue, market share, market segment domination, price leadership, technological superiority, a reputation for product quality—all represent benefits toward which cost incurrence can be directed. Costs generally follow from the kind of benefits desired and the level and type of activity necessary to achieve them.

Value Engineering. Within the benefit framework above, however, some analysis can yield a balancing of cost elements that is consistent with objectives. One approach to this analysis is value engineering or value analysis. Among the approaches found in value analysis are such things as:

- finding or developing the least-expensive materials or methods consistent with the operating requirements of the product or service;
- incorporating in the design or service only the quality needed to assure the benefits planned;
- making an effort to balance the useful life and the function of components so as to achieve a uniformity in design consistent with the period of obsolescence or depreciation of the product.

An example of value engineering is the substitution of a plastic part of less-expensive manufacture for a metal part that exceeds the normal use requirement of the product. Another example is the shift from large standard copper automobile radiators of high cooling capacity to smaller aluminum radiators sufficient only to cool a vehicle in normal use (perhaps satisfying the needs of 95 percent of the total number of users). Those wishing to tow trailers or drive regularly in mountains or deserts are advised to order additional cooling packages at extra cost. Such steps may aid in holding costs down to avoid price increases, increase production efficiency, facilitate the flow of work, or provide other benefits. Costs required to meet the extra needs of some users of the product or service can be offset by added charges only to those who require the extras.

Product Redesign. As in cost reduction, effecting a program of product redesign can be a part of cost optimization. A product can be upgraded to appeal to a higher-priced segment of the market, or downgraded to move to a lower-priced and higher volume market. The cost consequences of either kind of redesign are intended to result in an improved profitability, if successful.

Another aspect of product redesign may be simply to facilitate the fabrication and assembly process rather than to reposition the marketing strategy of the organization. Small changes in methods of casting, forging, or stamping metals; changes in fasteners—screws, rivets, bolts, and the like; and revised sequences of production activities, such as reversing painting and assembling operations, can often yield an improvement in the structure of costs.

Finally, costs can be restructured to some extent by organization redesign. A change from functional to project management or matrix management, or a flattening of the organization hierarchy, or a decentralization of management, or the introduction of the profit center or investment center concept in place of a cost center responsibility are examples of organization redesign that can have a salutary effect on costs.

CONCLUSIONS

There are limits to achieving control over costs through approaches such as cost planning, cost control, cost reduction, and cost optimization. Ultimately, the human element is a major determinant of the degree of success attainable by the means presented in this chapter.

Efforts to manage cost factors should be consistent with the organization's objectives and plans. The proper dimension of control should be identified and communicated to those responsible for operations. Control activities oriented to the wrong cost control dimensions may delay the resolution of problems and might possibly jeopardize the success of other areas of performance. If action is taken to reduce costs, when control of costs is desired, results can range from inferior product quality, through reduced maintenance and inadequate support activity, to unplanned organizational and technological experimentation.

A strong organizational commitment to good cost planning and control principles by the board of directors and management will convey to everyone the fact that rationally controlling costs is viewed as important and therefore not to be done haphazardly.

NOTES

1. The following material is slightly modified from an article by the author: John P. Fertakis, "Some Dimensions in the Management of Costs," *Managerial Planning*, September/October 1984, pp. 45–49.

2. Vilfredo Pareto, *Manuel d'economie politique* (Paris: V. Giard and E. Briere, 1909). Translated by Ann S. Schwier, *Manual of Political Economy* (New York: Augustus M. Kelly, 1971). Note especially Chapter 7, pp. 281–319.

3. Alfred L. Hunt, "Cost Reduction—How and Where to Apply It," *Selected Papers* (Haskins and Sells, 1968), pp. 425–440.

4. R.S. Edwards, "The Rationale of Cost Accounting," *LSE Essays on Cost* (London School of Economics and Political Science), 1973, pp. 87–88.

5. Hunt.

6. Wickham Skinner, "Boosting Productivity Is the Wrong Focus," *Wall Street Journal*, March 15, 1982, p. 26.

CHAPTER 11

INVESTING AND FINANCING DECISIONS: STRUCTURING THE BALANCE SHEET

Among the major proposals brought to the board of directors by management are those relating to financing activities and investing activities. In general, financing activities are those related to obtaining resources and repaying the providers of those resources. Investing activities include lending and collecting loans, and acquiring and disposing of securities and productive assets. Operating activities are the third major area of decisions likely to come before the board. These are discussed throughout this book (see especially Chapters 6–9 and Chapter 12). They involve production, personnel, marketing, and short-term financial decisions relating to the ongoing business of the organization.

The Statement of Changes in Financial Position, or Funds Statement, is a report that highlights these three major decision categories. As the board of directors considers financial performance, it may be instructive to review the recapitulation of its major approval and oversight functions provided by the Statement of Changes. Board members might ask themselves how many of these decisions involved their participation or approval. And they might ask management why they were not consulted if that is the case.

THE NEED FOR FINANCING

Business organizations exist because a need exists. When a sufficient number of people want something, a market develops in which those who have or can produce a good or service can meet those who want it. If some effort is required to extract or produce the product, an investment must be made in the required resources. Alternative methods for financing the investment must be considered. Financing decisions have the effect of restructuring the liability and stockholder equity portions of the balance sheet.

In the typical case the financing of an organization is provided by owners. This is more than a loan because owners receive no guarantee of repayment or interest. As a business grows it may require additional financing, such as the sale of more ownership shares, or borrowing. Borrowing can take the form of issuing long-term securities such as bonds for cash, obtaining property with a mortgage obligation, or signing promissory notes with lenders in exchange for cash or other resources. On a shorter term basis, some financing is obtained by credit terms with suppliers to allow a delay in payments for supplies and inventories. A wide variety of other short-term and long-term borrowing arrangements are available. Also included in the area of financing decisions are the payment of dividends to stockholders and the repayment of borrowing obligations.

One would expect that a business firm would avoid debt and arrange all financing with owners, but there are compelling reasons to pursue debt financing. Owners may not wish or be able to make added investments in the firm. The cost of borrowing funds (interest) may be lower than the dividend expectations of owners. Owners may benefit by borrowing funds at a lower rate of interest than the rate of profitability of the funds when used in operations. Borrowing can meet short-term operating capital needs and be easily eliminated by repayment when the need for the funds has ended. Loans may not require the approval of directors or industry regulators or holders of other debt instruments of the firm. Finally, interest payments on borrowed funds are tax deductible expenses while dividends to stockholders are not.

For a variety of reasons, financing may take the form of sales of the company's own equity securities. Selling shares of unissued common stock or preferred stock can produce significant funds for capital investment purposes. If investments can produce a return greater than that required for dividends, there are advantages to this permanent capitalization. The firm avoids interest payments that would have to be paid on borrowed debt even if profits did not materialize. There is no maturity date on which equity securities must be paid off. With a higher ownership equity on the balance sheet, the firm may be in a better position for an increase in future debt financing, paving the way for even more funding for additional projects. For example, a firm with debt of $1 million and equity of $2 million has a 50 percent debt-to-equity ratio and may not be able or wish to exceed that rate. By increasing equity to $3 million, the debt ratio decreases to 33 percent, making the firm more attractive to lenders.

There are some drawbacks to the sale of equity securities that may be important considerations. The common stockholders' right to maintain their pro rata investment share requires that a more complex procedure be followed, in which current shareholders may have to be given rights to buy the added share offering. Approval of the board of directors and probably of the shareholders at large may have to be secured. Approval for the distribution of additional shares may have to be secured from the state of incorporation and the stock exchanges on which the company's stock is traded. The presence of new stockholders may also weaken the control of corporate affairs by the original shareholder group. Finally, dividend payments to shareholders are not tax deductible as are interest payments to lenders.

Under most circumstances, financing obtained from the sale of equity securities should not be used for short-term investments and operations. When the need for the funds ends, or when the investment ceases to be viable or profitable, it is difficult to eliminate the added outstanding stock and its dividend requirements. Debt, on the other hand, can usually be retired at the discretion of management or at maturity.

Long-term financing decisions should almost always be subject to review and approval by the board of directors. The board represents the stockholders and any financing decision affects the relative status and claims of the shareholders relative to the organization.

INVESTING

Investing decisions have the effect of structuring the assets of the organization. The business must have a location, usually evidenced by land and buildings. It usually does something—requiring equipment to move goods or manufacture products. (In an operations sense, the business must invest in people, organization, inventories and supplies, and other operations-related things. Operations are considered a separate category and are discussed in Chapter 9.)

Investments

Some typical major investment categories are: the purchase of property, plant, and equipment; the acquisition of another business; the purchase of securities of other firms; and making loans to other businesses. This category also includes the opposites: receipts from the sale of investments in property, plant, and equipment; sale of a unit of the business; sale of securities held as investments; and collection of loans made to others.

Investments are made to secure the most effective use of, and return on, the resources of the enterprise. Most investments support the primary functions of operating the business, but some are made to achieve other objectives. An accumulation of cash is not productive at all and should be employed in such a way as to achieve a return until needed for a longer-term purpose. Thus it is invested or loaned to others at some rate of interest. A manufacturer would not be expected to hold long-term investments in securities or other assets that are not related to its primary operations. The director should question the purposes of decisions to make such investments.

Leases

Leases represent a unique aspect of financing and investing. A lease can be viewed as a rental agreement that obligates both the property owner and the renter to a longer term and a more detailed arrangement. In some cases, however, the lease has become in effect an instalment purchase arrangement. If the term of the lease is the effective useful life of the asset or if the present value of the lease payments is near the current purchase price of the asset, then the lease has served only to disguise ownership. Such a rental arrangement is in reality an investment decision coupled with a financing decisions and should thus be reviewed by the board of directors in that light.

Generally accepted accounting principles now require that leases be classified as either operating leases, which are effectively rental arrangements, or capital leases, which are to be treated as asset purchases. If a lease meets the terms of being a capital lease, the asset must be recorded on the books of the lessee and the related long-term liability be shown at the present value of the payments. (See Chapter 7 for a further discussion of this topic.) Both aspects are to be reflected in the Statement of Changes in Financial Position as investing and financing activities, in a supplemental section of the report.

While operating leases can be viewed as operations decisions under management's responsibility, capital leases should certainly be viewed by directors in the same manner as other means of raising capital or other long-term investment alternatives. In many respects, capital leases may not give the firm the flexibility of outright asset ownership, and may involve other legal obligations that can become problems in the future.

ARE FINANCING AND INVESTING NEEDED?

Management proposals for financing and investing should come before the board of directors for review and oversight, if not for approval. Financing decisions involving long-term debt or equity securities *must* be approved by the directors. Other financing and investment decisions *should* be subject to board approval. As a general rule, the board should feel that it has participated in decisions regarding all reported financing and investing items on the Statement of Changes in Financial Position.

At times, management proposals may be questionable. An investment proposal for a new plant facility may be linked with a financing proposal to provide the needed funds. If an existing plant is idle or underutilized or unprofitable, a new plant may not be the only way to secure the desired result. Some proposals coming before the board may be based on esoteric considerations such as image or prestige. Replacing an existing computer that is doing its work satisfactorily may be nothing more than a desire to have a state-of-the-art installation that gives prestige to the director of computing operations.

The board should be satisfied that there are no hidden assets that are feasible alternatives to new investments, and that alternatives have been adequately considered. The board member might well ask what alternatives were rejected in connection with an investing and financing proposal, and for what reasons. Staff reports to management on various proposals should be available for review. If none exist, one might well be suspicious about the homework that wasn't done in the decision process.

FORECASTS

Investment and financing decisions should be supported by forecasts. These are generally based on projections of factors in the organization's environment that are expected to impact future operations. Investments tend to involve the acquisition of resources to be used in operating the business. Financing arrangements produce needed funds and require future payments of dividends to stockholders or interest to creditors. In the latter case, the organization is also expected to provide for the repayment of the principal from resources provided by the operations that were financed.

A forecast is a projection of what is expected to happen in the future. A weather forecast, for example, is based on measurements of past and current conditions and the projection of the most likely weather pattern to evolve from those conditions. The forecast allows one to take steps to protect property and prepare for the future. Similarly, business forecasts signal operating and financial steps appropriate to expected future economic and other conditions.

Two general approaches are used in business forecasting. In one approach, which can be called the trend approach, the basic assumption is that the organization operates in a condition of relative stability. That is, the conditions that have determined the environment of the organization in the past will continue into the future. Thus a forecast can be based on trends revealed by past observations. If a cost factor has increased 5 percent each year for several years, and there is no evidence of changes in the environment in which that cost occurs, a 5 percent increase in the cost can be planned for the ensuing year. If a plant facility must be replaced and construction costs have been increasing steadily as measured by construction indexes, one may project the investment required in two years and incorporate the trend percentages in the financing plan.

Revenue, too, can be forecast by projecting marketing data from past trends of units sales and prices. It is important under the trend method to be alert to changes in the factors that underlie the assumption of stability. For example, a firm with a product line oriented to infants might be caught by surprise if it does not watch for changes in yearly demographic data on population birth rates and infant mortality.

The second approach to forecasting is that the organization must determine the key factors that affect its operations and attempt to forecast each one to arrive at an overall plan. In this view, the causal factors view, change is taken as a fact of life and many factors must be studied to determine how the future will be affected. It is common to look at such major areas of innovation and change as social, technological, and natural factors.

Social factors include cultural, economic, and political forces. Changes in consumer confidence, consumer tastes, public concerns, attitudes, incomes, national priorities, and other areas can have a significant effect on business operations. Organizational change may also be viewed as a social change. Technological factors include developing concepts and practices in science and engineering. Examples include scientific discovery, invention, innovation, the development of new methods and new products, and technology-induced problems that often create the need for ever more technology. Natural factors might include catastrophe, discovery, and evolution. For example, fire, flood, earthquake, weather, and climatic changes can have severe impacts on organizations. Unfortunately, the ability to forecast these factors is still somewhat limited, though some progress is being made. Much of the effort to cope with natural forces still rests on insurance, and that in itself is a significant forecasting factor.

The organization that has incorporated a forecasting frame of reference is in a much better position to develop alternatives for accommodating expected changes. Change itself creates the possibility for innovation—the development of new approaches, new strategies, new products, the shaping of public opinion and preferences, and other possible ways to confront change and turn it to the organization's advantage.

A board of directors that finds itself making financing and investment decisions on a hurried or crisis basis is being poorly served by its management. The absence of alternative strategies or time in which to consider options thoroughly signals potential problems for the organization that go beyond the decision itself. The need to replace equipment immediately or to expand operations or to borrow funds places the directors at risk and encourages a crisis atmosphere for decision making. The board should expect an executive group that looks to the future, develops forecasts, makes plans that allow adequate lead times for making decisions, and presents alternatives for consideration by the board. One may well argue that the board should not decide among courses of action but merely approve the plan proposed by management. However, the oversight responsibility of the director cannot be met without considering the reason for a decision and reviewing its benefits over other possible decisions.

DECISION CRITERIA

Adequate forecasting and planning allow the development of criteria for making investment and financing decisions. Criteria are standards or expectations that guide the selection process and aid in decision making. A broad criterion for an investment in machinery might be that it improves company profitability, or decreases dependence on an unreliable source of supply, or that the funds invested must be recovered within a given time period. A machine costing $100,000 that saves $20,000 a year in the cost of producing a product has a five-year investment recovery (payback) period. The criteria relating to profitability and payback period represent quantitative measures that permit comparisons with other projects that are competing for funds. The criterion relating to a dependable source of supply represents a qualitative criterion that makes choices a little more intuitive.

A common criterion for judging investments is the frequently used accounting-derived book rate of return. It is widely used because this criterion ties in closely with the rate of profitability that is important to stockholders— that which appears on the Statement of Income. Using the machine example above, if a 20 percent rate of return is the criterion (sometimes called a hurdle rate), the investment would be justified since a $20,000 annual benefit on an investment of $100,000 is 20 percent per year.

Another common investment criterion, one that takes into consideration the number of years that the asset is expected to be used, is the discounted rate of return. Assuming that the machine has a ten-year useful life, one would calculate the rate that would discount annual cash flows of $20,000 for ten years to a present value equal to the investment cost of $100,000. That rate is 15 percent and the investment would not be justified using the criterion of a 20 percent return on invested funds. Note that this investment will save $200,000 over its ten-year life, but the discounting technique places a decreasing value on cash flows as they become more distant into the future. Many feel that the discounted cash flow technique—the present value method—is a more theoretically sound basis for investing decisions.

The payback criterion is frequently used in cases where there is a high degree of risk associated with the investment or where the firm has cash flow problems that require a rapid return on projects so that other projects may have funds available. It is, in fact, the most common investment criterion as a first screening of potential projects, if not the sole criterion. Other criteria may place a limit on the dollar amount available for investment, provide for operational priorities of various kinds, or limit the purposes of investments in some way.

Criteria involving rates of return sometimes are based on the weighted average cost of capital. That is, an investment must produce a return greater than the cost of all sources of funding rather than only the cost of the specific financing proposed. Such a hurdle rate assures that stockholders will benefit from the investment.

Financing plans, too, can be subject to various criteria. For example, an interest rate ceiling may be imposed. This could be a fixed rate such as a policy allowing no borrowing at interest rates above 12 percent, or above a benchmark such as 2 percent above the prime bank lending rate. In general, financing availability is subject to so many external factors that a firm must remain flexible and seek the best rate available at the time of the decision.

Financing plans involving equity securities (stock) may be subject to limitations and criteria of a wide variety. For example, a corporate charter may limit the total shares of capitalization. Stock exchanges may impose limitations in stock offerings. The state in which the corporation is chartered may impose taxes on increased share authorization, or may limit opportunities to amend the corporate charter to permit the additional issuance of shares. Banks may impose loan covenants that restrict the proportion of debt to equity that a firm may show on its Statement of Financial Position.

The board of directors should inquire into the types of criteria considered by management in its proposals for investment and financing activities. It may of course impose criteria of its own, or modify those currently in use. In the case of new product research or other developmental projects, qualitative or goal-related criteria may be called for. The U.S. penchant for short-term profitability goals is viewed by many analysts as an impediment to innovation and competitiveness in the future.

A crisis investment decision such as repairing a worn out leaky roof or obsolete or broken down machinery does not permit the employment of an effective policy or the development of alternatives. But such decisions represent a flaw in management planning and forecasting. These events should have been anticipated and provided for as investment and financing proposals before they became a crisis situation. The return on such investments is infinite since there will be *no* return on operations if the investment is not made. Similarly, such decisions rarely offer time to look for the best financing arrangements. Bank borrowing at prevailing rates is all that is usually feasible under emergency circumstances. If internally available resources are used, the firm forgoes the return that the funds could have earned had they been invested or used in other ways.

CONCLUSION

One writer has identified nine major nonroutine decisions that are frequently encountered at higher levels in business organizations:

1. New product
2. Distribution channels
3. Acquisitions
4. Disinvestment (product abandonment)

5. Capital expenditures
6. Lease-purchase
7. Make or buy
8. Pricing
9. Manpower planning[1]

It is evident that this list of frequently encountered higher management decisions is heavily weighted by operational decisions. Items 3, 5, and 6 can be considered investing decisions, and financing decisions seem to be absent from this list. But this is not surprising: Financing decisions ought to be infrequent occurrences.

Many decisions are made within corporate operations that are in effect investing and financing decisions that are short-term in nature and do not normally require oversight by the board. Budgets are usually the first glimpse of short-term financing and investing decisions made at this level. In the strict sense, every operating plan involving the use of organization resources is an investment decision, and every source of funds involving bank loans or credit purchases is a financing decision. These tend to be tactical and involve relatively short-term operations time periods. Through policies regarding spending and borrowing authority, limits on amounts that can be spent or borrowed, and other managerial and financial controls such as budgets, the board can delegate, yet oversee, such decisions and allow the operations people the flexibility to meet emerging problems and opportunities.

It is unfortunate that major operating decisions are not highlighted in a statement like the Statement of Changes in Financial Position. In the typical statement, the operations component is a reconciliation from the reported accrual accounting income to the cash flow generated from operations. This should highlight the major thrust of the corporate board review and oversight function: operations. Such decisions are in fact reported only in summary fashion in the bottom-line profitability figure in the Statement of Income. Only the minutes of board meetings or committees will show what decisions were approved; and nowhere will there be a routine formal accounting of the results of such decisions individually.

It is not uncommon for questions about operations to dominate the agenda at annual stockholders' meetings. Board members, while supporting their officers and management, might be alert to discussions of operating decisions and review what part, if any, they played in the approval of such decisions.

NOTE

1. Lawrence A. Gordon, Danny Miller, and Henry Mintzberg, *Normative Models of Managerial Decision Making* (New York: National Association of Accountants, 1975).

CHAPTER 12

THE DIRECTOR AND FOREIGN OPERATIONS

There is a tendency to think of international business and trade as the realm of the very large business organization. In actuality, businesses of all sizes may find themselves engaged in commerce across national boundaries—which makes them international business organizations. The motivation for going international varies, but in the usual case the firm either desires a product or service not readily available in its own country or is available at lower cost elsewhere, or it finds that there is greater market demand or the opportunity for more profitable sales in other nations. Another reason for buying or selling in other countries might be to smooth out the cyclical nature of activities by buying or selling in nations with different seasonal business patterns.

Foreign operations create problems of organizing, managing, planning, budgeting, financing, reporting, evaluating, and controlling that are beyond what one would experience in operations that are solely domestic. The director should be aware of the added complexity introduced by different social, cultural, political, economic, taxation, and legal systems when an organization is international.

TERMS

Three terms often used when speaking of international business should be clearly understood before proceeding further. An international business can be illustrated by a firm organized in the United States (domestic operations or the parent organization) that buys or sells products overseas in the course of its domestic operations. It may in this endeavor own foreign organizations that can be autonomous and self-sustaining within the host country. The parent company may be primarily interested in obtaining profits or in obtaining products or in selling in that market. In restricted economies such as the European Common Market or the Association of Southeast Asian Nations (ASEAN) market, it may be desirable to have goods produced by a foreign subsidiary under the control of the parent organization.

A multinational business differs in concept because the U.S. firm retains ownership or control of production or service facilities within other countries, which are fully integrated in a parent company environment that now includes foreign extensions. The international business treats its overseas operations as outside transactions, while the multinational firm views transactions as being within the structure of the parent company as a whole. A transnational organization utilizes economic as well as political factors to optimize its position with regard to production, sales, and services on a global basis without regard to national boundaries or domestic/overseas distinctions.

IMPORTANCE OF FOREIGN OPERATIONS

In U.S. multinational firms, almost 34 percent of consolidated income was due to their foreign subsidiaries in 1985.[1] The benefits of overseas operations can be seen in the 10 percent profit on every dollar of sales overseas compared with 8 percent on domestic sales. The stronger returns on both sales and assets are attractive inducements to expanding business operations overseas. The 1985 results reported by Business International were obtained despite sluggish overseas growth and a strong U.S. dollar that limited sales for that year. U.S. firms invested $131 billion overseas, which brought the total U.S. investment to $1.2 trillion.

Some reasons for extending the organization's environment outside its home country are: (1) to offset cyclical sales performance patterns in the United States, (2) to gain a presence in a controlled economic area such as the Southeast Asian nations or the European Common Market, (3) to avoid strong competitive factors at home, (4) to meet rising worldwide demand that has outpaced the local economies' ability to produce their own goods and services, (5) to take advantage of low production costs overseas, and (6) to attain rapid growth that is more difficult in a mature economy.

HOW DOES IT HAPPEN?

Involvement with foreign trade and investment may start quite inadvertently. At first, perhaps an inquiry about the firm's product or an offer to buy is received from a foreign company or government. Such an opportunity is attractive because sales overseas tend to be profitable and such sales have no effect on regular domestic sales of the company's product. A single, lump-sum transaction and the opportunity for longer and more efficient production runs can lead to important economies of scale.

Problems arise, however, as the details are worked out. An evaluation of the credit rating of a foreign buyer may be difficult. The economic and political stability of the foreign firm and its country must be evaluated. Some questions arise in several areas. Are financial statements and accounting methods creditable? Is the currency stable or volatile? Is the sale to be denominated in U.S. dollars or in the foreign currency? How will the goods be shipped and insured? Who will arrange export and import licenses, legal documentation, and permits? How will payment be made? Which banks will handle the transactions and the conversion to U.S. dollars? What happens if currency exchange rates change during the term of the agreement?

The employment of a consultant or broker to handle the complexities of foreign sales and deliveries will add some costs, but a beneficial outcome will be more likely. Conversely, the above process may arise not from a sale, but from a need to purchase a good overseas because of scarcity or cost advantages. In either case, the firm has become an international organization. This first step easily leads to the next.

As the volume of foreign sales or purchases grows, it becomes attractive to organize a separate department that can reduce reliance on outside consultants by developing such expertise within the firm. The organization tends to more aggressively pursue sales and sourcing of goods overseas as this talent grows and business horizons broaden. Many attractive opportunities arise and must be screened for decisions. At this point, tax considerations tend to become important factors for consideration. A special export or import company may evolve from the internal department as tax breaks can be derived from having a Domestic International Sales Corporation (DISC) or other arrangement. The need then arises for special accounting systems and procedures for reporting, control, and tax purposes. A separately incorporated division to conduct international transactions can also have the benefit of reducing the potential financial liability of the U.S. firm if things go wrong.

The third stage comes as confidence develops and success is achieved in foreign sales and purchases. A move toward establishing foreign *operations* is a logical step. Again, various degrees of involvement are possible. At one extreme, a foreign manufacturer may be licensed to produce the product being imported or to sell products from the U.S. firm in that country. At the other extreme is the full ownership acquisition of a firm that becomes the subsidiary of the U.S. parent company. Between these opposites are such arrangements as the establishment of sales offices, warehouses, and joint ventures with foreign partners.

Each of these possibilities requires special considerations for accounting, information systems, finance, manufacturing, marketing, management, controls, and governmental relations. A large multinational firm may have an annual budget larger than the entire economy of some countries in which it operates. The potential for abusing such an economic power is great and the consequences would be far-reaching in importance for the firm and for the United States.

SUCCESS FACTORS IN INTERNATIONAL OPERATIONS

Success in international operations requires attention to information systems, organization structure, and controls beyond the operations themselves. Each of these features must be designed to conform to the requirements of the situation in which the firm finds itself. They must also be coordinated with the philosophy and systems of the U.S. parent organization. Among the influences to be considered are:

- The degree of management centralization
- The style of management (authoritative or democratic)
- The emphasis on functions versus products versus geography
- The methods used in planning and goal setting

Information systems, organization structure, and controls must interact with each other and with the operating environment of the firm as a whole. One indication of a failure to accomplish a good balance here is the number of crises or unanticipated problems encountered by management and the board.

Information Problems

Foreign operations may be distant in two important respects: geographic and cultural. Communication costs may be quite high because of the distance and the need to preserve the confidentiality of information. The need for two-way conversations that assure complete understanding will sometimes result in long telephone calls, and sometimes in the necessity for people such as auditors, operations specialists, experts, and managers to travel and personally meet with overseas personnel.

Employees who are foreign nationals must not only be trained in prescribed operating procedures, but they may also require indoctrination in basic U.S.

values and culture. The work ethic itself may have to be communicated and impressed upon indigenous employees and managers. The importance of time, of being prompt in arriving for appointments, of keeping records, of following policies, and of being consistent may be foreign to local people. These can be problems if the conduct of business in the host country is a matter of family or of who one knows, not what one knows.

Another information-related problem is the increased number of people and government entities who must be provided with information. A business must report to the public, shareholders, creditors, labor organizations, and government entities of a wide variety. One adds a new set of each in each country in which the firm operates. Additionally, a new currency, a new set of tax rules, new accounting requirements, and a different language and cultural perspective in the meaning of common terminology must be accommodated.

Even the name of the company, its trademarks, and its product brands can have unexpected meanings or connotations when transposed to a foreign setting. For example, the meaning of the term *Nova* in South American countries means "won't go" and is hardly a suitable brand name for an automobile being exported to that area. Funds spent in researching linguistics can help avoid such pitfalls but raise the cost of entry into a foreign land.

Organization Issues

The way in which an organization arranges its components for management, coordination, communication, and control is important for its success. Lines of authority and degrees of responsibility may be highly structured in some organizations, while in other such matters are adapted to the uniqueness of each part of the firm. However, the organization as it is shown on paper may be quite different from the way it really operates. When the firm extends itself to other countries such differences may be more critical.

Figure 12-1
Organization Chart with a Foreign Sales Division

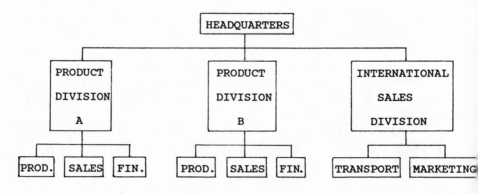

Figure 12-2
Organization Chart Illustrating a Product Orientation

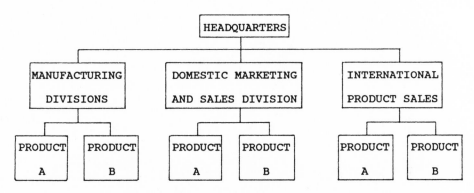

In the case of an international division status for a foreign operation, most functions remain centralized. Proven expertise is available from the staff and other managers in the domestic operations. Disputes may arise, however, on scheduling of production and deliveries, required modifications of products (110-volt versus 220-volt appliances for example), and the prices charged by the domestic production operations and staff to the foreign division (setting a transfer price for goods and services provided by one organization unit to another). Figure 12-1 illustrates the foreign operation as a sales division serving various producing divisions that carry out the full functions of production and sales. Figure 12-2 illustrates a functional approach in which some domestic divisions produce various products and others sell them. The foreign sales division brings international expertise to the sales of each product overseas.

The foreign operations may each handle one parent company product or the full range of products in overseas purchases, sales, and services. A frequent result of the foreign sales division status is that the division must compete with and be subservient to a domestic division's ability and willingness to give due priority to the foreign division's requirements. The primary relationships for domestic operations are with each other. They know each other and communicate frequently. A foreign division may be viewed as a way to get rid of excess goods produced or a way to employ excess plant capacity. Management must assure that the objectives of foreign operations are clear and that they are serviced accordingly.

The advantage of a single-product foreign sales division is the greater expertise and market development focus that is attainable. This is desirable for a highly technical product or one that requires a high level of service. A disadvantage of the single-product division is the need for multiple sales outlets, offices, and staffs in a given country—one for each product.

The multiple product division can of course be more efficient in that only one division is required in each country. A product approach in which the foreign

Figure 12-3
Organization Chart with a Full-Function International Division

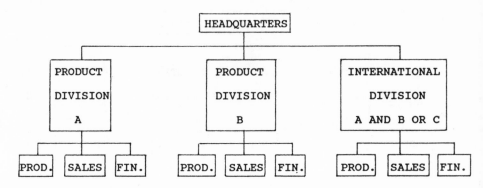

division carries out the full range of functions with respect to each product (production, sales, and finance) is shown in Figure 12-3. A multinational or transnational firm would probably have such an organization, and may in fact locate its production facilities centrally to serve sales in many countries. Foreign divisions may also be administratively grouped by geographic area to take advantage of specialized knowledge of the region's people, economy, culture, and politics. Figure 12-4 illustrates a geographic emphasis in a company's operations.

There can be many variations in the organization patterns of firms with foreign divisions. The selection of a specific type of organization configuration

Figure 12-4
Organization Chart with a Geographic Orientation

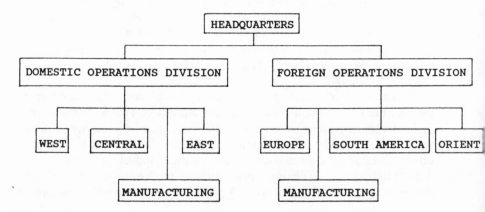

is related to where the expertise exists, where plants are operated, the number and complexity of products and markets, the culture and politics of each region, and the purposes of entering foreign environments.

The evaluation of product performance, division performance, and management performance in foreign divisions must be consistent with the purpose of the activity and with good management motivational principles. For example, if the price for international purchases and sales between divisions is set by the headquarters office, it is inappropriate to hold the division manager responsible for the profitability of products or the division. There should also be an understanding about whether performance is to be evaluated in terms of standards in the host country or those attainable in the United States. For example, if U.S. firms average a 15 percent return on invested capital, but a 20 percent return is average in the host country, which will be used for evaluation purposes?

Some common administrative perspectives for foreign operations are ethnocentric, polycentric, and geocentric. In the ethnocentric perspective, the domestic (U.S.) way of doing things predominates. In this view, everything is done best as it is done at home. The dominant concern is the contribution of the foreign division to sales and profits of the parent as measured in U.S. dollars. The polycentric perspective recognizes the need for diversity and autonomy in the foreign operation. There are few parent company controls and financial results are evaluated in the foreign currency and in the context of the host country's business environment. In the geocentric or global perspective, all organization units are seen as elements in a worldwide strategy. Decisions are based on global concerns regarding sales, costs, taxes, risks, and so forth. For example, products are made where costs are least, sales are made where profits are highest, and income is ideally reported in a country where taxes are lowest. In effect, the parent company is only an element in the worldwide enterprise, and it is considered an equal to those in other countries. The firms that adopt this perspective are truly multinational or transnational rather than being merely international.

Control Issues

Foreign operations are distant, communication is impersonal and expensive, and language, culture, and currency differences abound. It is not surprising then that the most common controls over foreign operations are financial, budgetary, and statistical in nature. They are strongly influenced by the parent organization and tend to differ very little from those used in domestic operations. Controls generally take the form of treating foreign operations as profit or investment centers, with return on investment as the primary performance measure.

Distant operations and complex arrangements tend to create top management anxiety, which often culminates in plant visits overseas by officers and directors. While little can be achieved by such visits, it seems important to show the flag and reiterate the rules of the game. As in any inspection, the purpose is to remind everyone of the policies and operating procedures instituted by the parent and get the place in order. A more effective control is the visit by operations line managers of the domestic divisions who have the expertise to discuss operating matters properly with their counterparts. A traveling internal audit staff is also an effective control in that they assure that the information base upon which many decisions are founded is in good order and that reports can be relied upon.

At times there seems to be an ambivalence about the degree of control the parent should exercise over its subsidiary. Decentralization of operations management control relieves the parent company management of responsibility for complex transactions and involvement in operating problems. The foreign unit is allowed to function quickly and in a manner consistent with the local cultural, economic, and political environment. As the subsidiary becomes more autonomous, some uneasiness develops, or some economic setback may occur, and the parent begins to recentralize decision authority. Organizational objectives and strategies, too, may change or shift emphasis to other aspects of performance and central management dominance may reassert itself. This waxing and waning of headquarters dominance can be confusing or unsettling but is a fact of life in multinational organizations.

Paradoxically, as operations-level decisions are decentralized, management control should be even more centralized. Standards of performance and the measurement of performance should be consistent and well understood by all levels of the organization hierarchy. Japanese firms have focused on central management control of finance, accounting, and personnel training functions. This approach maintains the goal orientation and cultural, social, and economic perspectives of Japan in foreign operations while allowing adaptation to local conditions on a day-to-day basis.

A perhaps disturbing aspect of control for managers of foreign operations is the increasing dominance of the finance function in the decision-making process. The management of foreign capital investments, international fund transfers, taxes, and currency exchange risks makes a centralized management of such matters seem imperative. The complex process of hedging such risks and managing pools of various currencies is costly and inconsistent when left to the finance director of each subsidiary. Therefore centralization of control is almost inevitable and often unpopular with overseas managers. The transfer price mechanism for measuring transactions among operating units may be designed in some cases to report income in countries with low taxes or lax collection procedures or easy repatriation of funds to the parent organization. This of course shifts the return on investment to meet tax and other objectives and may conflict with the management evaluation and bonus systems. It may be necessary to restructure goals and measurement criteria to promote rational decisions.

Many countries impose laws and policies on such elements as currency movement, the import or export of products and components, the employment of local nationals in management positions, the setting of transfer prices, the imposition of requirements for licenses, permits, fees, and other items. There may be a requirement regarding technology transfer to assure national development in the host country's economy and the training of management infrastructures to assure future economic progress.

Peter F. Drucker has pointed out some factors leading to a decrease in the autonomy of foreign operating units of multinational firms.[2] First there is the inability of some national economies to absorb the output capacity of a modern production facility. These plants then are serving widespread markets in several countries from a single location. Second, markets have become global and less differentiated by culture and geography, making centralized decisions more feasible and efficient. Third, financing, investing, and capital spending decisions are being centralized to control risks as discussed above. In short, few operating divisions operate wholly within one nation's boundaries in all functions. Almost every major decision is thus a joint decision that is coordinated by the parent company. Drucker notes that, increasingly, management people have to become transnational. Advancement opportunities in such companies are no longer confined to moving up the corporate hierarchy in a single organization unit.

Herbert C. Knortz, former controller at ITT Corporation, places a high emphasis on managing risk in connection with foreign operations.[3] Any evaluation of foreign subsidiaries must factor in the element of risk through higher expected rates of return than is considered adequate for domestic divisions.

When establishing a foreign subsidiary, a lower level of risk can be attained by minimizing the equity investment of the parent organization. This means that much of the financing should be arranged by debt to local banks in the currency of the foreign country if reasonable terms can be arranged. The desire for new industry to bolster the economy may prompt a favorable borrowing climate. But Knortz notes that in the final analysis, it is the astute management of assets themselves that provides the greatest risk control. Among other operating controls, the firm should also strive to

- keep inventories at low levels
- keep receivables current and at a low level
- keep a low commitment in capital equipment
- remit excess cash to the parent as rapidly as possible
- borrow heavily in local currencies for working-capital needs
- lease or rent assets locally with lease payments to be made in local currencies
- establish pricing policies that incorporate high interest rates
- maintain sales prices consistent with price movements in the local economy
- assure that revenue increases from sales price increases are not fully absorbed by local employees and suppliers[4]

Local managers should produce translations of their financial reports into U.S. dollars using U.S. generally accepted accounting principles where they are different from those of the host country. They should review and evaluate their operating results in these terms to give them a more headquarters-oriented view of their achievements. Reports and statements should be forwarded to the parent company with appropriate notes, explanations, and comments.

Though it may seem attractive to form a foreign subsidiary with some minority equity (ownership) interest by local investors as a part of the effort to reduce risk, Knortz notes that it may not be desirable to do so. The decision process is slower and some resistance to various policies of the U.S. parent usually evolves. Conflicting goals and interests and evaluation criteria impede a good relationship. The pressure for an equal or even a dominant ownership interest and control by the local investors may manifest itself in the form of new laws to that effect, which may doom the venture to failure.

COMMON PRACTICES

Certain areas of consistency have been shown to be desirable in international enterprises. (The term is used here in its generic sense, including multinational and transnational firms.) To the extent that these can be incorporated in the policies and methods employed, the organization will benefit. Smith lists these areas as follows:

1. There should be a worldwide set of corporate policies and objectives that guide all management and operations.
2. The firm should have a uniform, worldwide chart of accounts and detailed explanations of each classification.
3. There should be uniform procedures for annual budgets and multiyear projections of operations.
4. A standard procedure should be used for preparing capital expenditure programs and requests.
5. Debts incurred and the current status of indebtedness should be frequently reported.
6. A close monitoring of exchange risk exposure, dividend planning, developing foreign tax credits, insurance coverage, and the economic and political stability of the host country should be conducted.
7. Prescribed monthly, quarterly, and year-end closing schedules for financial and statistical data should be established.
8. All financial reports should be adjusted to U.S. generally accepted accounting principles and adjusted for currency exchange rates before being transmitted to the parent organization. A written interpretation of reports in both local and U.S. terms should accompany the reports.[5]

SUMMARY

This chapter has emphasized the nature of international business, its opportunities and risks, and the controls that promote a successful integration of foreign operations with those of the parent organization. Increasingly, international experience and knowledge are required in the selection of chief executive officers of major business organizations. Similarly, knowledge of the control function is deemed highly desirable. Developing goals that transcend national boundaries and cultural differences and assuring a steady stream of relevant and reliable information about progress toward those goals are major executive roles.

AREAS TO MONITOR

Some international perspectives should also be developed in corporate directors. Some relevant areas to monitor or question might include:

- What company products or services are obtained from or sold to firms in other nations? Are these operations profitable, and what percentage of consolidated income is from international units of the organization?
- To what extent are important decisions such as finance, personnel, production, and marketing in foreign subsidiaries centralized under U.S. management?
- What are the major risks that the firm faces in its international operations and what steps have been taken to control such risks?
- Are any payments made to foreign nationals who are not contractors or employees of the firm?
- Are all resources and profits of foreign subsidiaries available for repatriation to the United States, and if not, what restrictions are there?
- Is the firm involved in partnerships or joint ventures from foreign-controlled organizations? Does the firm have a dominant or controlling position with respect to such arrangements?
- What products, if any, are bought from or sold to foreign governments?
- Are there any national security, social, or "rights" issues in connection with investments or income involving foreign countries?
- What problems or risks have been dealt with by management in the past two years involving foreign operations? How were these resolved?

NOTES

1. The figures cited here are from Business International's annual profitability survey as reported in the *Journal of Accountancy*, December 1986, p. 108.
2. Peter F. Drucker, "The Changing Multinational," *The Wall Street Journal*, January 15, 1986.

3. Herbert C. Knortz, "Controllership in International Corporations," *Financial Executive*, June 1969, pp. 54-58. Material in the following paragraphs has been excerpted from this article.

4. Ibid., p. 58.

5. Adapted from Willis A. Smith, "International Operations and Translation," in Lee J. Seidler and D.R. Carmichael, eds., *Accountants' Handbook*, 6th ed. (New York: John Wiley, 1981), Vol. 2, Section 39, p. 39-12.

CHAPTER 13

ANNUAL AND OTHER MEETINGS OF DIRECTORS

The annual meeting of stockholders is an opportunity for face-to-face accountability of corporate officers and directors to those who elect them. In the legal sense, holders of common stock have certain rights, among which are:

- The right to share pro rata in distributions of dividends.
- The right to maintain their relative share of ownership.
- The right to examine the books of the corporation.
- The right to elect directors.
- The right to vote on significant issues that come before the board, usually defined in the Articles of Incorporation, in the corporate bylaws, and in the laws of the state in which the organization is chartered.

Three stockholder rights that are of importance in the context of financial management and accounting are the right to examine the books of account, the right to vote on directors, and the right to vote on issues. The right to vote is often accomplished by proxy voting, in which each common stockholder is sent a ballot to be returned by mail. The vote for or against nominated directors and the vote to adopt or reject proposals on major issues such as compensation plans for officers and directors are accomplished through the proxy for those shareholders unable to attend the annual meeting. One vote is counted for each share of voting stock held.

The right to examine the books of account is met by mailing each stockholder an annual report consisting of financial reports and other data of interest. The annual report to shareholders has in many cases evolved into additional sections including a message from the president or chairman, a review of operations, summarized operating and financial data, and material on the members of the board and on executive officers of the corporation. With pertinent data distributed and the means for casting votes in the hands of stockholders, one may ask what is accomplished by holding the annual stockholders' meeting at which relatively few holders of stock are able or willing to attend.

GENERAL SHAREHOLDER QUESTIONS

The ritual of the annual meeting is in the best tradition of democratic institutions. The meeting is often required by law, but attendance by shareholders is not. This permits those with concerns and questions to voice them and receive a response from those whom they have elected to represent their interests. The opportunity for personal participation in discussions and voting is highly valued by many in our society.

The meeting generally includes social amenities such as plant tours, meals, receptions, and/or demonstrations of company products. In addition, presentations may include industry forecasts, new product introductions, and public relations matters of a wide variety. The focus, however, is the dialogue between share owners and officers and directors. Reference has been made elsewhere to common concerns and questions posed by shareholders. The Price-Waterhouse report entitled *Shareholders' Questions* classifies the wide variety of questions commonly asked as follows:

- Board of Directors (selection, activities, compensation)
- Corporate Accountability (auditing, internal control, information systems)
- Compensation (management pay, stock options, pension plans)
- Shareholder Matters (meetings, dividends, shareholder interests)
- Operations (general, corporate restructuring, foreign operations)
- Liquidity and Capital Resources
- Mergers, Acquisitions and Dispositions
- Financial Reporting and Accounting
- Taxes
- Legal Matters and Contingencies

- Corporate Responsibility (social, political, environmental, employees)
- Future Prospects[1]

Large corporations actively traded on organized stock exchanges frequently attract activist shareholders to their annual meetings. In such cases, questions are likely to focus on specific areas in great depth, such as the selection of directors, officers' compensation, corporate responsibility, foreign operations, or legal matters. But for most corporations, questions center on financial disclosures and operations and tend to be information-gathering in nature rather than being antagonistic.

A recent survey notes that only 3 percent of respondents named the annual report of the corporation as their best source of investment information.[2] The annual report has been criticized as being overly optimistic and too dominated by public relations concerns. Hence, the annual meeting presents the opportunity for delving into areas that stockholders may feel are slighted or misrepresented.

Among the accounting and financial reporting questions to be expected at annual stockholder meetings are the following examples, which are selected from the categories presented in the Price-Waterhouse compilation.

Accounting

- Does the company follow accounting practices prevalent in its industry?
- Why did the company change its method of accounting for _____? Why is this new method preferable to the old method?
- In light of SEC criticism of several companies' revenue recognition practices, please describe our company's recognition policies.
- Has the company considered adopting LIFO [last in, first out]? What would be the effect on earnings?
- Why were the actuarial assumptions used to determine pension costs changed?
- The annual report reflects fourth-quarter changes in estimates. What steps are being taken to prevent similar adjustments in the future? Why were these adjustments not recorded earlier?
- What caused the increase (decrease) in the _____ account compared to the prior year?
- What is the company's cash flow per share?
- What is the current value of the company's real estate?
- The return (on net assets) includes the effects of inflation whereas the net assets are at historical cost. What does this calculation yield if you use the current cost of net assets?

Reporting

- Why did the independent accounts qualify their report?
- Why are certain footnotes (e.g., quarterly financial data) in the financial statements labeled "unaudited"?

- Has the SEC commented in any way on the company's financial reporting? Are any SEC enforcement actions pending?

- Does the company have any unconsolidated subsidiaries (leasing, finance) or other special-purpose entities that provide financing to the company? What is the amount of this "off-balance-sheet" financing?

- Why isn't segment information provided in the quarterly reports to shareholders?

- What risks and uncertainties is the company exposed to? Why are these not disclosed in the financial statements?

- What is the book value per share of common stock? Why isn't it disclosed in the annual report?

- Are there any proposed FASB [Financial Accounting Standards Board] or SEC pronouncements that would significantly affect the company's financial statements?

The range of questions that shareholders ask can be seen to reflect not only the typical concerns of those who have entrusted their wealth to others, but also topics that tend to reflect more current developments. The average director would not be expected to be cognizant of many of these issues or company positions, but their very diversity illustrate the possible responsibilities for far-reaching review, oversight, and control issues. A conscientious director may want to reflect on who on the board is asking these questions of management between the annual meetings.

INTERACTIONS

Among officers and directors that should be present at the annual meeting to provide responses to such questions should be the controller and the treasurer and the chief financial officer. All members of the board of directors should of course be present—especially those on the audit commitee. The president and chief executive officer should be present as well as officers at the vice-presidential level.

In spite of the occasional confrontation at annual meetings, most such events are friendly and most people leave with a good feeling about their organization. Directors and officers tend to demonstrate solidarity and mutual support on such occasions. Challenges and differences of opinion among directors and officers are rare at annual meetings. This may not be the case in a corporation with troubles such as losses or declining profits, pending legal actions, declining sales, labor problems, or financing difficulties. While solidarity among the board members and corporate officers is especially important at such times, stockholders may feel that their officers and directors are not forthcoming and honest in their presentations and answers. Many questions will focus on the last topic in the question areas reported by Price-Waterhouse, future prospects.

PROMOTING CHANGE

The principal recourse of the disgruntled stockholder is to vote his or her stock for other than management-supported candidates for directorships, and against ballot proposals put forth by the board and management. A proxy fight is an attempt by dissident directors or a stockholder group to solicit shareholders' votes for their candidate or their side of a vote on a proposed course of action. Annual meetings have been known to be scheduled in hard-to-reach places in order to avoid having a large attendance when controversial issues must be considered. Another option for an unhappy stockholder is to sell his or her stock. Legal action is, of course, another possible recourse.

Attempts to replace incumbent directors or to counter a proposal by the board or to litigate an issue are seldom successful. The board should be a marketplace of ideas in which good ideas, introduced with tact and with relevant facts and information about problems and issues, should win out over poor ideas and proposals. For this reason, more effective change efforts may require the director's staying with the corporation and working for change from the inside—and avoiding confrontational tactics.

Attempting to introduce changes at board meetings and in operating policies is a daunting task. The term "good old boy" network is especially applicable to corporate directors and managers. Board meetings may take on a country club character, and are in fact often convened in posh surroundings, with food and drink and entertainment, with expensively bound copies of reports, with professionally prepared audio visual materials, and with conviviality as the rule.[3]

Some interesting observations are provided by Milton Lauenstein concerning the manipulation of the board of directors. He advises one who desires an impotent board to

make every effort to emphasize that the board is an elite group. The setting of the meetings, the quality of food and drink provided, and the format of material presented should all help promote the feeling that the body is above indulging in controversy or dealing with grubby commercial issues.

No opportunity should be missed to reinforce the directors' belief that they are the statesmen of the business community dealing with global issues and broad philosophical questions. Above all, the unwritten law that directors should not criticize each other or the company should be clearly recognized and enforced.[4]

THE AGENDA

The agenda is a strong control tool in the hands of a chairman or a CEO.[5] The agenda is often set by the chairman of the board and usually in conjunction with the CEO's advice. Rules of order for the conduct of meetings may make it difficult for individuals to introduce new topics that are not on the agenda.

A 1946 survey found no uniform practices with regard to meeting agendas.[6] Many companies did not furnish board members with advance copies of the agenda. Those that did send advance copies varied in time from two to four days before the meeting to one firm that sent it ten days in advance of the meeting. Without having the agenda in advance or having time to study it and any accompanying information, the director cannot effectively participate in deliberations on important issues coming before the board. A minimum agenda should include:

- The reading and approval of the minutes of the previous board meeting
- A treasurer's report
- Committee and staff reports
- Unfinished business from previous meetings
- New business about which information has been given out in advance
- The open opportunity to introduce new topics of concern or to ask questions. (Some organizations prefer that this item be omitted in favor of asking for an inclusion on a future agenda so that the required information can be gathered and sent to board members in advance.)

In the atmosphere of most board meetings it is not considered appropriate to introduce harsh elements of difficult or controversial questions, disagreement, or challenge. One who detracts from the convivial formality of the meeting may find his or her influence diminished, communications channels may be closed, and information and access to those who have information may be limited.

CONCLUSIONS

If the board of directors meets quarterly (which is a minimum number of times for effective board influence over management) or monthly, the annual meeting may be the fifth or thirteenth time the board has convened. Patterns of participation established in the past are not likely to change at the annual meeting. If change does occur, it is likely to be toward even more solidarity and less dissent in the presence of the company's constituent groups.

The director who wishes to remain effective must somehow tread the line of conformity and compliance on the one hand, which establishes him or her as a colleague among other directors, and the line of exercising individuality and responsibility on the other hand, which can lead to better organizational performance and to beneficial change. An overly docile director is open to liability for not keeping appropriate reins on management decisions and actions. In contrast, a director who exercises his or her conscience, asks the hard questions, and keeps well informed about matters of review, oversight, and control, will not likely be found negligent (and thus liable) when things go wrong.

When one accepts a corporate directorship, one accepts a great deal of responsibility. That responsibility often entails making important judgments and decisions on the basis of unfamiliar sources of information such as accounting reports and professional specialists of a wide variety.

Almost all important business decisions have financial effects that will be reflected in accounting reports. It has been the objective of this book to help the director who is unfamiliar with financial accounting processes and reports, and those who are new to the board of directors environment, to understand these systems and their relationship to underlying organizational processes.

NOTES

1. Excerpted from the table of contents, *Shareholders' Questions* (New York: Price-Waterhouse, 1987), p. 3. Other questions listed in this chapter are adapted from the same source.

2. Ned Raynolds, "What Investors Want from the Annual Report," *The Wall Street Journal*, January 18, 1988, p. 12 (citing a survey by Hill and Knowlton).

3. Harold M. Williams, "Corporate Accountability and Corporate Power," a paper presented at the Fairless Lecture Series, Carnegie Mellon University, Pittsburgh, October 24, 1979, pp. 7-8.

4. Milton C. Lauenstein, "Preserving the Impotence of the Board," *Harvard Business Review*, July-August 1977, pp. 36-37.

5. Harold M. Williams, "Corporate Accountability—One Year Later," *SEC News*, January 18, 1979.

6. Paul E. Holden, Lounsbury S. Fish, and Hubert L. Smith, *Top Management Organization and Control* (Stanford, Calif.: Stanford University Press, 1946), p. 230.

APPENDIX:
SUNDSTRAND CORPORATION
ANNUAL REPORT FOR 1986:
FINANCIAL REVIEW SECTION

To our Stockholders:

Financial Highlights

(Dollar amounts in millions except per share data)

	1986	1985	Percent Change
Net sales	**$1,433.9**	$1,284.1	+ 12%
Orders received	**$1,446.2**	$1,467.3	– 1%
Unfilled orders	**$1,066.2**	$1,053.9	+ 1%
Net earnings	$ **45.4**	$ 74.4	– 39%
Earnings per share	$ **2.42**	$ 4.02	– 40%
Dividends per share	$ **1.80**	$ 1.80	No change

1986 earnings did not meet the $4.50 per share forecast we made at the April annual meeting. At the end of the third quarter this forecast was lowered to $4.10 per share as a result of the impact of the Tax Reform Act, along with the lack of recovery in industrial markets. In addition, the Company recently decided to reserve $31.7 million net or $1.69 per share against 1986 earnings for the ultimate resolution of government contract disputes. Although we have not conducted settlement discussions with the government, the Company feels adequate provision has been made for resolution of the disputes and related costs.

Aerospace sales increased steadily throughout 1986. Deliveries for the B-1B program, growth in the Turbomach product line, continued healthy earnings in the commercial side of the business, and a solid aftermarket, all benefitted our aerospace business. The outlook for this business segment continues to be positive, with our strong market position in many major commercial and military programs. With the previously-mentioned government contract disputes, and grand jury investigations believed to involve allocation of costs to government contracts, Sundstrand has implemented changes in its procedures to minimize future disagreements between the Company and the government. Further changes are planned during 1987.

The Industrial business segment, in contrast, did not fare as well. Virtually all of our principal markets, which are dependent on industrial, energy, agriculture, and construction activity, were weak. These markets are expected to be weak for the near term. We believe, however, that the Industrial segment markets we serve play vital roles in the world's economies and will continue to provide worthwhile business opportunities over the long term.

Our Hydraulic Power Systems business, part of our Industrial segment, is a supplier of components and subsystems to manufacturers of off-highway mobile equipment. For several years the production of vehicles has been shifting from North America to the rest of the world. In order to be more effective in worldwide production and marketing, effective January 1, 1987, we established a joint venture with our European licensee, Sauer Getriebe AG of Neumuenster, West Germany, combining their business with our Hydraulic Power Systems business.

Sundstrand and Sauer each own 50% of the joint venture, which operates 12 manufacturing facilities worldwide. Our license agreements for the manufacture of hydraulic power system products in other world territories have been assigned from Sundstrand to the joint venture so that it can operate on a truly worldwide basis. This important step recognizes the increasingly global dimension of the off-highway vehicle industry and puts the new company in a particularly good position to serve major producers.

In support of Sundstrand's commitment to market leadership and corporate permanence, in 1987 we plan to spend $130 million for property, plant, and equipment and $113 million for research and development. A strong balance sheet, which is integral to our market leadership strategy, enables us to budget these amounts.

During 1986 our debt to total capital ratio declined from 35.2% at the beginning of the year to 34.4% at year-end. The strength of our balance sheet enabled us to achieve an investment grade rating of A when we issued $100 million of 9-3/8% 30-year debentures during the second quarter of 1986. The debt issue, due serially from 1997 to 2016, extends our level debt maturity schedule.

Stockholders' equity increased during the year by $15.5 million to $604.7 million, after payment of $1.80 dividends per share. The Company has paid dividends to its shareholders for 171 consecutive quarters.

We are pleased with the long-term effects of the 1986 Tax Reform Act on our business. On the other hand, we are concerned about the potential for damage to our international markets resulting from the continued pressure in Congress for new and restrictive trade laws. We will continue expressing our views on risks associated with such legislation.

We have long practiced integrity at Sundstrand — integrity toward our employees, toward our suppliers, and toward our customers. Earlier this year we distributed to all employees a new Code of Business Conduct and Ethics handbook, which reflects that practice of integrity. We believe in the Code. It is important to us, to our employees, to our suppliers, and to our customers. We are proud of our history of integrity as a Company, and believe our renewed commitment will make Sundstrand an even better corporate citizen.

Sundstrand welcomes Harry C. Stonecipher to the Sundstrand Corporation Executive Office. Mr. Stonecipher joined Sundstrand January 1, 1987, as Executive Vice President.

James Wm. Ethington, Retired Chairman of Sundstrand Corporation and a Director for 28 years, will be retiring from the Board of Directors this year. We wish to recognize Mr. Ethington's excellent leadership of this Company, and his many contributions to our continued success.

We also thank our employees, stockholders, vendors, and customers for their continued support during 1986.

Sincerely,

Evans W. Erikson
Chairman of the Board
and Chief Executive Officer

Don R. O'Hare
Vice Chairman of the Board

David MacMorris
Executive Vice President

Harry C. Stonecipher
Executive Vice President

March 11, 1987

Financial Review

Increased demand for Sundstrand's military and commercial aerospace products resulted in higher sales during 1986. Sundstrand's Industrial units continued to operate during 1986 at depressed levels. Earnings in 1986 include a loss provision of $61.5 million before income taxes and $31.7 million after income taxes ($1.69 per share) for the ultimate resolution of government contract disputes in the Company's Aerospace business segment. The Company's financial position remains strong after making this provision, and the major cash acquisitions of Turbomach in 1985 and Sullair Corporation in 1984. Recent trends are discussed on this page and should be read in conjunction with the financial data, charts, and commentary presented elsewhere in this Annual Report.

Sales

Sales in 1986 of $1,433.9 million were 11.7% above 1985. Sundstrand's Aerospace business segment was responsible for this increase.

	Sales increase (decrease) from prior year		
Business segment	**1986**	1985	1984
Aerospace	**20.1%**	24.3%	14.3%
Industrial	**(2.6%)**	21.5%	15.0%
Total	**11.7%**	23.2%	14.6%

Aerospace sales reflect a 108.5% growth in military shipments and a 36.4% growth in commercial shipments since 1982. Demand for Industrial products has been depressed for the last five years. The Aerospace sales growth in 1985 and 1986 has benefitted from the acquisition of Turbomach in midyear 1985 and Industrial sales comparisons include the acquisition of Sullair Corporation in late 1984.

Earnings

Operating profits totaled $100.6 million in 1986 compared to $152.1 million in 1985. The loss provision for resolution of government contract disputes in the Aerospace segment and reduced sales and margins in the Industrial segment were the primary reasons for this earnings reduction. Without the loss provision, Aerospace operating profits would have increased $24.2 million over 1985. Aerospace profit margin excluding the loss provision was 16.1%, down slightly from 1985 due to higher company-funded research and development expenses, partially offset by the benefits of higher sales volume. Profit margins for Aerospace in 1985 were higher than 1984, reflecting the benefit of higher sales and an increase in commercial aftermarket shipments. Higher sales caused Aerospace margins to improve in 1984 over 1983, despite increased expenses related to new military programs.

Profit margins for the Industrial segment have been low for the past five years due to depressed market conditions. Following an improvement in Industrial margins in 1984 over 1983 due to improved sales, 1985 margins dropped, reflecting lower shipments of heat transfer surfaces, reduced margins on sales of hydraulic power products, and the change to the LIFO method of valuing certain subsidiaries' inventories. Another drop in Industrial margins occurred in 1986 due to lower sales and reduced margins on sales of mechanical power transmission products, hydraulic power products, and compressors, partially offset by improved margins on sales of heat transfer surfaces.

	Operating profit as a percent of net sales			
Business segment	**1986**	1985	1984	1983
Aerospace (a)	**9.7%**	16.3%	15.2%	14.9%
Industrial	**1.4%**	4.3%	6.7%	2.2%
Total	**7.0%**	11.8%	12.0%	10.1%

(a) Operating profit as a percent of sales for Aerospace for 1986 excluding the loss provision for resolution of government contract disputes was 16.1%.

Higher sales, acquisitions, new military program expenses, and increased company-funded research and development costs caused marketing and administration expenses to rise $47.0 million in 1986, $57.7 million in 1985, and $29.8 million in 1984. Research and development expenses were $124.9 million ($66.4 million from Company funds and $58.5 million from customer-sponsored projects) in 1986 compared to $100.6 million in 1985 and $98.8 million in 1984. The Company has budgeted $113.0 million for research and development in 1987, including $54.0 million of Company-funded expenditures. Interest expense, net of interest and dividend income, was $30.0 million in 1986 and $25.3 million 1985, substantial increases over the prior two years, due to two large cash acquisitions which were partially funded by increased debt. Earnings per common share for 1986 were reduced by approximately $.20 due to the 1986 Tax Reform Act, which, in the long term is expected to result in higher earnings for the Company because the benefit of lower tax rates is expected to exceed the loss of tax credits.

The Company has paid cash dividends every year for the last 42 years. Regular quarterly dividends were paid at the rate of 45 cents in each quarter for the last five years for a total of $1.80 for each year.

The Company believes that, on the average, selling price increases have approximated cost increases during 1986. Inflation also affects the Company's assets and liabilities. Since Sundstrand's monetary assets (cash and receivables) are less than its monetary liabilities, assuming continued inflation, the Company will achieve some future benefits by paying its fixed debts with dollars that have decreased in purchasing power. Inventories at Sundstrand are valued using principally the first-in, first-out (FIFO) method. Since costs have not been rising rapidly during recent years, the amount by which cost of products sold has been understated has been smaller than during a period of rapidly escalating costs. Certain subsidiaries of the Company switched to the last-in, first-out method of inventory valuation during 1985.

Sundstrand could not replace its property, plant, and equipment today for the historical cost value at which they are carried on the books. Many technological advances have occurred since these assets were acquired and therefore the Company doubts that it would ever replace existing assets with carbon copies of its present property, plant and equipment. The Company's use of accelerated depreciation methods for tax purposes partially compensates for the cash flow impact of inflation on property, plant, and equipment.

The Company anticipates overall improvement in its Aerospace segment sales during 1987 as a result of increasing commercial aviation activity. Industrial segment activity is expected to remain flat during the first half of 1987.

Government Contract Disputes

Sundstrand has received final decision letters from a Government Administrative Contracting Officer regarding alleged noncompliances with Cost Accounting Standards and Federal Acquisition Regulations for the years 1978 through 1985. The government has informed Sundstrand that it intends to pursue collection of approximately $13.9 million plus interest resulting from these alleged noncompliances. Sundstrand has appealed or plans to appeal these decision letters to the Armed Services Board of Contract Appeals.

Sundstrand has also received determination letters alleging noncompliance with Cost Accounting Standards and Federal Acquisition Regulations claiming approximately $106.4 million of misallocated costs plus interest for the years 1981 through 1985. If the government were to prevail in the claims made in these determination letters, the amounts owed by the Company could materially exceed $106.4 million plus interest since years other than those covered by the government's determination letters may contain similar alleged noncompliances. Other government contract disputes exist on which determination letters have not been received by the Company.

The Company was advised on July 16, 1986 and December 16, 1986 that it is the subject of federal grand jury investigations in the Northern District of Illinois and the Western District of Washington, respectively. The Company believes that the investigations involve allocation of costs to government contracts. Under government procurement regulations, an indictment or conviction resulting from either investigation could result in the significant impairment or termination of Sundstrand Corporation's ability to receive new government contracts and the imposition of materially adverse fines and penalties.

The Company has implemented changes in its procedures to minimize future disagreements between the Company and the government. Further changes are planned during 1987.

Fourth quarter and total year 1986 results included a loss provision of $61.5 million before income taxes and $31.7 million after income taxes ($1.69 per share) for the ultimate resolution of government contract disputes in the Company's Aerospace business segment. Although the Company has not engaged in settlement discussions with the government, it is management's opinion that adequate provisions have been made for the resolution of government contract disputes, which may involve litigation and take an extended period of time.

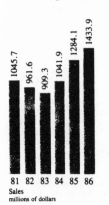

Sales
millions of dollars

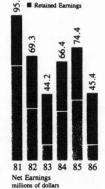

Net Earnings
millions of dollars

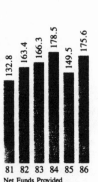

Net Funds Provided
by Operating Activities
millions of dollars

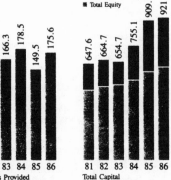

Total Capital
millions of dollars

Corporate Liquidity

The major uses of funds provided by operations and additions of property, plant, and equipment during the past three years are shown below.

	1986	1985	1984
		(Amounts in millions)	
Total funds provided by operations	$208.3	$174.3	$156.5
Changes in elements of working capital excluding acquisitions			
Accounts receivable	(4.1)	(8.3)	21.0
Inventories	(25.0)	(46.3)	(27.0)
Accounts payable and accrued expenses	(3.2)	30.0	28.6
Other	(0.4)	(0.2)	(0.6)
Net funds provided by operating activities	$175.6	$149.5	$178.5
Additions of property, plant, and equip., at cost	$111.5	$109.4	$ 93.2
Additions of property, plant, and equipment, net	$106.7	$103.9	$ 90.7

Following a decrease in 1984, accounts receivable rose by $8.3 million in 1985 and $4.1 million in 1986 due to higher sales partially offset by continued emphasis on collection and credit control measures. Until a current dispute with the government is resolved, collection of accounts receivable will be temporarily reduced. Inventories increased in each of the last three years as demand for Aerospace products rose. Since December 31, 1983, progress payments received have increased by $42.6 million. The increase in accounts payable and accrued expenses in 1984 was partially due to the cessation of pre-funding of certain retirement plan contributions that had occurred in prior years. The increase in accounts payable and accrued expenses in 1985 reflected higher Aerospace production levels. Additions at cost, of property, plant, and equipment of $111.5 million in 1986 exceeded depreciation by $40.9 million. Plans for 1987 call for capital spending of $130.0 million, of which $41.4 million was actually committed at December 31, 1986. The Company believes that present available capital resources plus funds provided by operating activities will be adequate to meet 1987 operating requirements.

Capital Resources

The Company's financial planning includes maintaining a sound relationship between stockholders' equity and total funds borrowed. The ratio of total debt to total capital on December 31, 1986 was 34.4% compared to 35.2% at the end of 1985 and 29.0% at the end of 1984. The acquisition of Turbomach caused this increase in 1985.

Sundstrand has a revolving credit/term loan facility providing revolving credit in the amount of $745.0 million during twelve months of the year comprised of a base commitment of $400.0 million and a back-up commitment of $345.0 million. Base commitment debt may be borrowed under the facility from the banks providing the revolving credit/term loan facility. Back-up commitment represents an obligation to refund borrowings other than those borrowed under the base portion of this facility. The Company may at any time convert some or all of the back-up commitment to base commitment. Revolving credit borrowings outstanding at November 30, 1989 may be converted at the Company's option to term loans maturing December 1, 1992. The Company also issues commercial paper at various times, which is supported by the back-up commitment in the revolving credit/term loan facility.

During 1984 Sundstrand raised $50.0 million in long-term debt to partially fund the Sullair acquisition. Another $50.0 million in long-term debt was raised in 1985 to partially fund the Turbomach acquisition. During 1986 the Company issued $100.0 million of sinking fund debentures, which was used to repay short-term indebtedness and for general corporate purposes.

Information by Business Segment

Financial data with respect to the various business segments in which Sundstrand operates is set forth below. Intersegment sales are immaterial. Military sales occur primarily in the Aerospace segment.

		(Amounts in thousands)	
	1986	1985	1984
Net sales			
Aerospace	$ 968,040	$ 805,883	$ 648,178
Industrial	465,900	478,258	393,770
	$1,433,940	$1,284,141	$1,041,948
The above includes:			
Sales from foreign operations			
to unaffiliated customers	$ 91,304	$ 80,046	$ 72,260
Export sales of domestically			
manufactured products	$ 239,939	$ 187,077	$ 160,688
Military sales (final customer is primarily			
the U.S. Government)	$ 594,468	$ 493,416	$ 408,573
Operating profit			
Aerospace (1986 includes $61,500,000 provision			
for resolution of government contract disputes)	$ 94,276	$ 131,631	$ 98,740
Industrial	6,346	20,487	26,341
Total operating profit	100,622	152,118	125,081
Interest expense	(56,349)	(38,825)	(25,322)
Interest and dividend income	26,299	13,539	13,469
General corporate expenses	(12,740)	(11,579)	(9,319)
Other	8,577	4,439	7,741
Earnings before income taxes	$ 66,409	$ 119,692	$ 111,650
Assets			
Aerospace	$ 907,359	$ 832,134	$ 588,470
Industrial	427,525	441,510	461,127
Corporate	64,292	37,535	40,283
	$1,399,176	$1,311,179	$1,089,880
Net additions to property, plant, and equipment			
(includes leased equipment)			
Aerospace	$ 92,088	$ 95,453	$ 73,517
Industrial	19,950	18,532	23,212
Corporate	2,383	(1,269)	3,236
	$ 114,421	$ 112,716	$ 99,965
Depreciation and amortization			
(includes leased equipment)			
Aerospace	$ 55,935	$ 44,324	$ 36,860
Industrial	27,402	26,391	24,223
Corporate	1,016	630	725
	$ 84,353	$ 71,345	$ 61,808

Consolidated Statement of Earnings

	(Amounts in thousands except per share data)		
	Year ended December 31,		
	1986	1985	1984
Net sales	**$1,433,940**	$1,284,141	$1,041,948
Costs and expenses			
Costs of products sold	**944,297**	850,460	688,375
Marketing and administration	**343,389**	296,379	238,654
Provision for resolution of government contract disputes	**61,500**	—	—
	1,349,186	1,146,839	927,029
Earnings before other income (deductions)	**84,754**	137,302	114,919
Other income (deductions)			
Royalties and commissions	**8,201**	5,534	4,112
Interest expense	**(56,349)**	(38,825)	(25,322)
Interest and dividend income	**26,299**	13,539	13,469
Unclassified, net	**3,504**	2,142	4,472
	(18,345)	(17,610)	(3,269)
Earnings before income taxes	**66,409**	119,692	111,650
Income taxes	**21,009**	45,244	45,238
NET EARNINGS	**$ 45,400**	$ 74,448	$ 66,412
Weighted average number of common shares outstanding	**18,733**	18,533	18,300
Earnings per common share	**$ 2.42**	$ 4.02	$ 3.63
Cash dividends per common share	**$ 1.80**	$ 1.80	$ 1.80

Consolidated Balance Sheet

	(Amounts in thousands)	
	December 31,	
Assets	1986	1985
Current Assets		
Cash and cash equivalents	$ 16,280	$ 2,704
Accounts receivable, less allowance for doubtful		
accounts of $4,011,000 in 1986 and $2,641,000 in 1985	200,926	196,876
Inventories, net of progress payments	427,412	402,403
Other current assets	24,800	19,097
Total current assets	669,418	621,080
Property, Plant, and Equipment, Net	505,142	469,119
Leased Equipment, Net	19,773	18,103
Intangible Assets	127,228	122,178
Other Assets (principally prefunding of		
group benefit programs)	77,615	80,699
	$1,399,176	$1,311,179

Liabilities and Stockholders' Equity		
Current Liabilities		
Notes payable	$ 8,221	$ 81,937
Long-term debt due within one year	12,182	12,911
Accounts payable	94,507	103,372
Accrued salaries, wages, and commissions	44,976	39,132
Contributions due retirement plans	25,884	22,738
Other accrued liabilities	69,441	72,781
Total current liabilities	255,211	332,871
Government Contract Disputes Provision	61,500	—
Deferred Income Taxes	181,034	164,027
Long-Term Debt (less current portion)	296,762	225,152
Stockholders' Equity		
Common Stock, par value $1; authorized		
50,000,000 shares; issued 1986—18,921,507 shares,		
1985—18,921,507 shares	18,921	18,921
Additional contributed capital	130,921	128,244
Retained earnings	476,774	465,117
Foreign currency translation adjustment	(7,152)	(8,365)
Treasury Common Stock at cost; 1986—166,001 shares,		
1985—254,138 shares	(5,705)	(8,651)
Unamortized value of restricted stock issued	(9,090)	(6,137)
	604,669	589,129
	$1,399,176	$1,311,179

Consolidated Statement of Changes in Financial Position

| | (Amounts in thousands) | | |
| | Year ended December 31, | | |
	1986	1985	1984
Operating activities			
Funds provided by operations			
Net earnings	**$ 45,400**	$ 74,448	$ 66,412
Depreciation of property, plant, and equipment	**70,670**	59,811	51,754
Depreciation of leased equipment	**6,058**	5,535	5,531
Amortization	**7,625**	5,999	4,523
Deferred income taxes	**17,007**	28,499	28,246
Provision for resolution of government			
contract disputes	**61,500**	—	—
Total funds provided by operations	**208,260**	174,292	156,466
Changes in elements of working capital			
excluding acquisitions			
(Increase) decrease in accounts receivable	**(4,050)**	(8,328)	21,009
Increase in inventories	**(25,009)**	(46,341)	(26,983)
(Decrease) increase in accounts payable	**(8,865)**	14,271	12,912
Increase in accrued expenses	**5,650**	15,794	15,705
Other	**(403)**	(149)	(569)
Net funds obtained from (used for) working capital	**(32,677)**	(24,753)	22,074
NET FUNDS PROVIDED BY OPERATING ACTIVITIES	**175,583**	149,539	178,540
DIVIDENDS PAID	**(33,743)**	(33,345)	(33,059)
Investing activities			
Additions of property, plant, and equipment, net	**(106,693)**	(103,915)	(90,675)
Additions of leased equipment, net	**(7,728)**	(8,801)	(9,290)
(Increase) decrease in intangible and other assets	**(13,257)**	4,174	1,934
Businesses sold	—	—	5,229
Businesses acquired			
Net current assets (exclusive of cash)	—	(26,077)	(37,127)
Net property, plant, and equipment	—	(40,381)	(18,051)
Other	—	(56,674)	(78,638)
NET FUNDS USED FOR INVESTING ACTIVITIES	**(127,678)**	(231,674)	(226,618)
Financing activities			
Debt transactions			
Issuance of long-term debt	**101,000**	79,672	50,000
Payments of long-term debt	**(30,119)**	(15,961)	(43,508)
(Decrease) increase in notes payable	**(73,716)**	36,976	18,065
Debt assumed from acquisitions	—	—	46,876
Equity transactions			
Acquisitions	—	—	12,416
Purchase of treasury shares	—	(2,274)	(11,230)
Stock issued for pension funding	—	9,983	—
Other	**2,249**	3,039	(723)
NET FUNDS PROVIDED BY (USED FOR)			
FINANCING ACTIVITIES	**(586)**	111,435	71,896
(Decrease) increase in cash and cash equivalents	**13,576**	(4,045)	(9,241)
Cash and cash equivalents at January 1	**2,704**	6,749	15,990
CASH AND CASH EQUIVALENTS			
AT DECEMBER 31	**$ 16,280**	$ 2,704	$ 6,749

Consolidated Statement of Stockholders' Equity

| | (Amounts in thousands) | | |
| | December 31, | | |
	1986	1985	1984
Common Stock			
Balance at beginning of year	**$ 18,921**	$ 18,704	$ 18,550
Stock issued for acquisition of Signatron, Inc.	**—**	—	154
Stock issued for pension funding	**—**	217	—
Balance at end of year	**$18,921**	$ 18,921	$ 18,704
Additional Contributed Capital			
Balance at beginning of year	**$128,244**	$117,674	$115,646
Stock issued for acquisition of Signatron, Inc.	**—**	—	35
Treasury stock issued for acquisition of			
Wulfsberg Electronics, Inc.	**—**	—	263
Stock issued for pension funding	**—**	9,766	—
Stock issued under employee stock plans	**2,677**	804	1,730
Balance at end of year	**$130,921**	$128,244	$117,674
Retained Earnings			
Balance at beginning of year	**$465,117**	$424,014	$389,221
Adjustment for pooling of Signatron, Inc.	**—**	—	1,440
Net earnings	**45,400**	74,448	66,412
Cash dividends paid	**(33,743)**	(33,345)	(33,059)
Balance at end of year	**$476,774**	$465,117	$424,014
Foreign Currency Translation Adjustment			
Balance at beginning of year	**$ (8,365)**	$(10,364)	$ (8,619)
Adjustment for the year	**1,213**	1,999	(1,745)
Balance at end of year	**$ (7,152)**	$ (8,365)	$(10,364)
Treasury Stock			
Balance at beginning of year	**$ (8,651)**	$ (6,589)	$ (7,825)
Purchase of 50,350 and 255,400 shares,			
respectively, for treasury	**—**	(2,274)	(11,230)
Stock issued for acquisition of			
Wulfsberg Electronics, Inc.	**—**	—	10,584
Stock issued under employee stock plans	**3,191**	233	2,057
Purchase of shares previously issued			
under restricted stock plans - 4,650, 440, and			
4,030 shares, respectively	**(245)**	(21)	(175)
Balance at end of year	**$ (5,705)**	$ (8,651)	$ (6,589)
Unamortized Value of Restricted Stock Issued			
Balance at beginning of year	**$ (6,137)**	$ (7,654)	$ (6,574)
Stock issued under employee stock plans	**(4,891)**	(46)	(2,717)
Purchase of shares previously issued			
under restricted stock plans	**127**	3	104
Amortization of deferred compensation			
under restricted stock plans	**1,811**	1,560	1,533
Balance at end of year	**$ (9,090)**	$ (6,137)	$ (7,654)

Financial Summary

Summary of Significant Accounting Policies

Principles of Consolidation provide for the inclusion of the accounts of Sundstrand Corporation and all significant subsidiaries. The financial statements of certain subsidiaries outside of the United States are included on a September 30 or November 30 fiscal year basis.

Inventories are valued at the lower of cost (principally first-in, first-out method) or market. During 1985 certain subsidiaries changed to the last-in, first-out method. Abnormal idle capacity costs are recorded as period costs and excluded from inventory values.

Property, Plant, and Equipment and Leased Equipment are recorded at cost and are depreciated principally on the straight-line method. Accelerated depreciation methods are used for tax purposes.

Investment Tax Credits are recorded under the flow-through method as a reduction of the current provision for federal income taxes.

Business Segment information is presented on page 24.

Inventories

The classification of inventories at December 31, 1986 and 1985, was as follows:

	(Amounts in thousands)	
	1986	1985
Raw materials	**$ 90,116**	$ 90,002
Work in process	**220,571**	251,447
Finished goods and parts	**225,483**	187,120
	536,170	528,569
Less progress payments	**108,758**	126,166
	$427,412	$402,403

During 1985, Sundstrand changed its method of valuing certain subsidiaries' inventories to the LIFO method for consolidated financial reporting. The change conforms the method of valuing inventories used to report to stockholders to the method used prior to 1985 for income tax reporting. The Company believes the use of the LIFO method for those subsidiaries more properly matches costs and related revenues. It is not practicable to determine either the cumulative effects of the change on retained earnings at January 1, 1985 or the proforma effects of retroactive application of the change for prior periods. In accordance with generally accepted accounting principles, the change to the LIFO method was prospective from January 1, 1985. The addition to the LIFO inventory reserve for 1985 was $3,647,000. The effect of the change for 1985 was to decrease net earnings from $76,271,000 to $74,448,000 or $.10 per share.

Inventoried costs relating to long-term contracts are stated at the actual production cost incurred to date, reduced by amounts identified with progress payments received. The costs attributed to units delivered under such contracts are based on actual costs incurred. Marketing and administrative costs are expensed as incurred. Long-term contracts are aggregated because of similarities in technologies used, development and application engineering, and manufacturing processes employed. When the current estimate of the long-term commitments indicates a loss will be incurred, such loss is accrued.

Property, Plant, and Equipment and Leased Equipment

The estimated useful lives used in computing provisions for depreciation follow:

Land improvements	20 to 25 years
Buildings	20 to 40 years
Building equipment and improvements	10 to 25 years
Machinery and equipment	3 to 20 years
Office furniture and fixtures	4 to 10 years
Leasehold improvements	Lease life
Leased equipment	3 to 7 years

Additions and retirements and the related accumulated depreciation are summarized as follows:

(Amounts in thousands)

	Property, plant, and equipment				
	Land and improvements	Buildings and improvements	Machinery and equipment	Total	Leased equipment
Cost					
Balances at December 31, 1983	$17,686	$122,697	$465,862	$606,245	$44,435
Additions at cost	866	11,658	80,681	93,205	9,351
Acquired companies	760	8,175	9,116	18,051	—
Retirements	(24)	(884)	(33,376)	(34,284)	(294)
Currency translation	(48)	(363)	(2,449)	(2,860)	—
Balances at December 31, 1984	19,240	141,283	519,834	680,357	53,492
Additions at cost	1,255	24,014	84,113	109,382	11,950
Acquired companies	8,332	3,945	28,104	40,381	—
Retirements	(361)	(643)	(28,589)	(29,593)	(19,946)
Currency translation	34	426	2,617	3,077	—
Balances at December 31, 1985	28,500	169,025	606,079	803,604	45,496
Additions at cost	2,584	27,548	81,407	111,539	7,728
Retirements	(293)	(4,497)	(9,876)	(14,666)	—
Currency translation	73	602	1,129	1,804	—
Balances at December 31, 1986	$30,864	$192,678	$678,739	$902,281	$53,224
Accumulated depreciation					
Balances at December 31, 1983	$ 3,934	$ 43,355	$227,642	$274,931	$33,357
Depreciation	521	4,620	46,613	51,754	5,531
Retirements	(28)	(536)	(28,760)	(29,324)	(233)
Currency translation	(6)	(173)	(1,459)	(1,638)	—
Balances at December 31, 1984	4,421	47,266	244,036	295,723	38,655
Depreciation	508	6,020	53,283	59,811	5,535
Retirements	(55)	(298)	(22,798)	(23,151)	(16,797)
Currency translation	6	562	1,534	2,102	—
Balances at December 31, 1985	4,880	53,550	276,055	334,485	27,393
Depreciation	530	6,178	63,962	70,670	6,058
Retirements	(99)	(1,158)	(7,759)	(9,016)	—
Currency translation	6	325	669	1,000	—
Balances at December 31, 1986	$ 5,317	$ 58,895	$332,927	$397,139	$33,451

Income Taxes

Income tax expense for the three years ended December 31, 1986, consisted of the following components:

		(Amounts in thousands)	
	1986	1985	1984
Current income tax expense (benefit)	$ 613	$(10,877)	$13,129
Deferred income tax expense	20,396	56,121	32,109
Total income tax expense	$ 21,009	$ 45,244	$45,238
Total income tax expense includes:			
State tax (principally deferred)	$ 2,789	$ 5,051	$ 4,784
Foreign tax (principally current)	$ 6,918	$ 7,243	$ 5,334

Deferred income tax expense resulted from timing differences in the recognition of revenue and expense for tax and financial statement purposes. The sources of these differences in each respective year and the corresponding tax effect of each were as follows:

		(Amounts in thousands)	
	1986	1985	1984
Differences in reporting income on long-term contracts	$ (4,963)	$(1,145)	$ (976)
Excess of tax over book depreciation	15,610	8,622	5,590
Undistributed earnings of foreign subsidiaries not considered permanently invested	50,824	44,549	25,953
Excess of book over tax provision for government contract disputes	(29,827)	—	—
Differences in tax and book employee benefit expenses	(7,771)	(2,783)	3,088
Miscellaneous other items	(3,477)	6,878	(1,546)
Total deferred income tax expense	$20,396	$56,121	$32,109

Total income tax expense for each respective year varied from the amount computed by applying the statutory United States federal income tax rate to earnings before income taxes for the reasons set forth in the following reconciliation.

		(Amounts in thousands)	
	1986	1985	1984
Income tax expense at 46%	$30,548	$55,058	$51,359
Increases (reductions) in taxes resulting from:			
State taxes based on income, net of federal income taxes	1,506	2,728	2,583
Investment tax credits	(2,064)	(6,123)	(5,090)
Taxes on subsidiaries at rates other than 46%	(8,508)	(8,396)	(5,767)
FSC and DISC tax benefits	(2,200)	(2,063)	(1,309)
Miscellaneous other items	1,727	4,040	3,462
Actual income tax expense	$21,009	$45,244	$45,238
"Effective" tax rate	31.6%	37.8%	40.5%

The Company's Singapore subsidiary has an export enterprise certificate whereby 90% of its export profits during the ten year period ending July 1, 1992 are exempt from tax. Aggregate (and per share) tax benefits attributable to these exemptions on amounts considered permanently invested were $5,450,000 ($.29) in 1986, $6,670,000 ($.36) in 1985, and $4,790,000 ($.26) in 1984.

Domestic and foreign earnings before taxes for the three years ended December 31, 1986, as shown below, exclude profits recorded on intercompany sales, and net interest expense is allocated between geographic segments based on assets.

		(Amounts in thousands)	
	1986	1985	1984
Domestic	$ 57,909	$111,021	$106,225
Foreign	8,500	8,671	5,425
Total earnings before taxes	$ 66,409	$119,692	$111,650

Total assets at December 31, 1986, of operations outside the United States were $97,982,000 after deducting $518,893,000 of notes and accounts receivable due from Sundstrand's domestic operations. Sundstrand's equity in its foreign operations was $556,399,000. At December 31, 1986, the Company has not provided federal income taxes on $132,287,000 of undistributed earnings recorded by certain subsidiaries outside the United States, as these earnings were deemed permanently invested.

Federal income tax returns have been examined and cleared by the Internal Revenue Service through 1976. The years 1977 and 1978 have also been examined, and all issues have been resolved, with the exception of two relating to intercompany transactions between Sundstrand Corporation and a foreign subsidiary for which the Internal Revenue Service has assessed the Company $7,500,000 (excluding interest). The Company does not agree with the Internal Revenue Service's position and has filed a petition with the United States Tax Court requesting redetermination of the deficiency. The Internal Revenue Service has issued its examination report for 1979 and 1980, which proposes assessments of $18.6 million and $23.8 million (excluding interest), respectively, with which the Company does not agree. Of these amounts, $18.4 million would result in reduction of taxes in years after 1980, and $23.5 million represents a continuation of the intercompany pricing issue discussed above. Operations of this foreign subsidiary have grown significantly since 1980 and, following examination, the Internal Revenue Service may assess additional taxes for these years. The Company currently provides deferred taxes on a substantial portion of the undistributed earnings of this subsidiary due to its intent to repatriate these earnings in the future. Based on final resolution of this matter, the Company may revise its intentions with respect to the repatriation of these earnings and, accordingly, management believes that the ultimate resolution of this matter will not have a material effect on the financial position or earnings of the Company. In the opinion of management, adequate provision has been made for all income taxes.

Notes Payable

The following table summarizes Sundstrand's short-term borrowing activity including commercial paper for the three years ended December 31, 1986.

| | (Amounts in thousands) | | |
	1986	1985	1984
Outstanding borrowing at December 31 (a)	$ 8,221	$ 81,937	$ 44,961
Short-term borrowing			
Daily average during year	$320,736	$180,296	$ 70,961
Maximum amount at any month end (b)	$413,709	$409,936	$263,544
Weighted average stated interest rate			
During the year	7.03%	8.95%	11.03%
At December 31 (a)	11.27%	8.52%	10.29%

(a) December 31, 1986 short-term borrowings are principally local currency borrowings by foreign subsidiaries.

(b) Unused committed credit facilities at these peak borrowing month ends were $154,826,000, $162,081,000, and $106,799,000, respectively, of which $154,826,000, $138,651,000, and $36,731,000, respectively, were available and permissible under the Company's most restrictive debt covenants. Cash and cash equivalent balances at these peak borrowing month ends were $348,668,000, $306,095,000, and $209,385,000, respectively.

At December 31, 1986, Sundstrand's short-term domestic borrowings were all supported by a revolving credit/term loan facility providing revolving credit in the amount of $745,000,000 during twelve months of the year comprised of a base commitment of $400,000,000 and a back-up commitment of $345,000,000 for a commitment fee of 1/4% and 1/8% per annum, respectively, on the average daily unutilized available credit. Revolving Credit borrowings outstanding at November 30, 1989 may be converted at the Company's option to term loans maturing December 1, 1992.

Long-Term Debt

The composition of long-term debt at December 31, 1986 and 1985 was as follows:

	(Amounts in thousands)	
	1986	1985
10.50% notes due serially to 1986-1991	**$ 28,800**	$ 33,600
11.05% notes due serially 1986-1999	**65,000**	70,000
12.50% notes due serially 1988-1992	**50,000**	50,000
12.00% notes due serially 1993-1997	**50,000**	50,000
9.38% Sinking Fund notes due 1997-2016	**100,000**	—
Other	**15,144**	34,463
	308,944	238,063
Less long-term debt due within one year	**12,182**	12,911
Long-term debt (less current portion)	**$296,762**	$225,152

Total principal payments required under long-term debt agreements for the five years subsequent to December 31, 1986, are $12,182,000 in 1987, $21,209,000 in 1988, $21,239,000 in 1989, $21,269,000 in 1990, and $21,595,000 in 1991.

The loan agreements contain certain restrictions with respect to the amount of retained earnings available for payment of cash dividends and acquisition of Sundstrand Common Stock. As of December 31, 1986 retained earnings exceeded the most restrictive of these provisions by $115,592,000.

On May 5, 1986 the Company issued $100,000,000 of 9.375% 30 Year Sinking Fund Debentures which are subject to a sinking fund of $5,000,000 face value in debentures annually beginning May 1, 1997. The Company has a non-cumulative option to triple each required payment. The Company may call and redeem these securities at any time at a price initially equal to 109.225% of face value and at prices declining to face value by 2006. Principal covenants include limitation on secured debt and on sale and leaseback of assets.

During 1981, a subsidiary of Sundstrand Corporation entered into an agreement whereby a third party assumed the repayment of the principal of $12,637,000 and interest on 8-3/4% sinking fund bonds due in 1987. Sundstrand is contingently liable until the third party discharges the assumed obligations.

Restricted Stock Plans

During 1986 and 1985, in accordance with the terms of the Sundstrand restricted stock plans, which were approved by the stockholders, 86,500 and 1,000 shares, respectively, of Common Stock were sold to key managerial employees at a price substantially below market price. This Common Stock may not be resold, except to Sundstrand, until the restrictions placed on these shares expire. The amount of compensation represented by the sale of restricted stock is being amortized over a nine-year vesting period. At December 31, 1986, 105,070 shares were available for granting under restricted stock plans.

Pension Plans, Post-Retirement Health Care, and Life Insurance

The Company has defined benefit pension plans covering substantially all United States employees. Pay related plans generally provide pension benefits that are based on the employee's highest compensation during a three-year or five-year period prior to retirement. Non-pay related plans provide benefits of stated amounts for each year of service. Pension plans for United States employees are funded at amounts greater than the minimum required by ERISA.

In the third quarter of 1986, the Company adopted Statement of Financial Accounting Standards No. 87, "Employers' Accounting for Pensions" (SFAS 87), for all United States pension plans, retroactive to January 1, 1986. Pension cost for these plans for 1986 and related disclosures, as of December 31, 1986, were determined under the provisions of SFAS 87. This change had no material impact on 1986 earnings.

Pension cost for 1986 included the following components:

	(Amounts in thousands)
Service cost of current period	$ 20,233
Interest cost on projected benefit obligation	37,194
Actual return on plan assets	(52,090)
Net amortization and deferral items:	
Amortization of initial benefit obligation	3,938
Deferred gain on plan assets	21,235
	$ 30,510

For 1985, pension cost of $30,724,000 was determined using the Frozen Entry Age Normal Method. Prior service costs were amortized over the estimated average remaining working lifetime of active employees. Prior service costs for non-pay related plans were amortized as a level dollar amount and such costs for pay related plans were amortized as a level percentage of pay. The assumed rate of return on plan assets was 8-1/2%. The actuarial present value of vested and non-vested accumulated plan benefits was $274,496,000 and $46,830,000, respectively, and net assets available for benefits were $329,189,000 as of January 1, 1985. Pension cost for 1984 was $27,363,000.

The funded status of the plans at December 31, 1986, was as follows:

	(Amounts in thousands)	
	Plans having assets which exceed accumulated benefits	Plans having accumulated benefits which exceed assets
Benefit obligation liability:		
Vested benefits	$(239,672)	$(53,512)
Nonvested benefits	(52,865)	(9,492)
Accumulated benefit obligation	(292,537)	(63,004)
Effect of projected future compensation levels	(99,140)	(28,714)
Projected benefit obligation	(391,677)	(91,718)
Plan assets at market value	372,096	56,131
Projected benefit obligation in excess of plan assets	(19,581)	(35,587)
Adjustments for deferrals of benefit obligation liability not yet recognized in pension cost:		
Net (gain) or loss due to variance of past experience from assumptions	(19,061)	3,714
Initial net benefit obligation liability to be amortized over average future service	25,271	30,311
Pension liability recognized in the balance sheet	$ (13,371)	$ (1,562)

The projected benefit obligation was determined using an assumed discount rate of 8-1/2%, and an assumed weighted average long-term rate of compensation increase of 7%. The assumed long-term rate of return on plan assets was 8-1/2%. Plan assets consist principally of common stocks and fixed income investments and include $38,418,000 of common stock of the Company at December 31, 1986 market value.

The Company provides health care and life insurance benefits for retired employees who become eligible for benefits, having satisfied certain age and/or service requirements. Health care and life insurance benefits are provided through insurance contracts or a group benefit trust. Premium and other payments totaling $4,451,000 and $3,869,000 for 1986 and 1985, respectively, are expensed as incurred. Health care and life insurance benefits for retirees of foreign operations, where applicable, are provided through government-sponsored plans to which the Company contributes, as required.

Supplementary Statement of Earnings Information

The items shown hereunder were charged directly to costs and expenses for the three years ended December 31, 1986.

	(Amounts in thousands)		
	1986	1985	1984
Maintenance and repairs	**$37,575**	$31,733	$31,490
Research and development:			
Company-funded	**66,439**	48,872	42,593
Customer-funded (Aerospace)	**58,447**	51,724	56,183
Rent and lease expense	**25,181**	20,206	15,555

The Company leases certain facilities and equipment under operating leases, many of which contain renewal options and escalation clauses. Minimum future rental commitments under noncancelable operating leases which extend beyond one year are payable as follows: 1987, $16,608,000; 1988, $11,285,000; 1989, $5,618,000; 1990, $2,183,000; 1991, $1,021,000; and after 1991, $1,406,000. Facilities and equipment under capital leases, minimum future rentals receivable under subleases, and contingent rental expenses were not significant.

Royalties, advertising costs, taxes other than payroll and income taxes, and amortization of intangible assets were each less than one percent of the total sales for each of the years.

Government Contract Disputes

Sundstrand has received final decision letters from a Government Administrative Contracting Officer regarding alleged noncompliances with Cost Accounting Standards and Federal Acquisition Regulations for the years 1978 through 1985. The government has informed Sundstrand that it intends to pursue collection of approximately $13.9 million plus interest resulting from these alleged noncompliances. Sundstrand has appealed or plans to appeal these decision letters to the Armed Services Board of Contract Appeals.

Sundstrand has also received determination letters alleging noncompliance with Cost Accounting Standards and Federal Acquisition Regulations claiming approximately $106.4 million of misallocated costs plus interest for the years 1981 through 1985. If the government were to prevail in the claims made in these determination letters, the amounts owed by the Company could materially exceed $106.4 million plus interest since years other than those covered by the government's determination letters may contain similar alleged noncompliances. Other government contract disputes exist on which determination letters have not been received by the Company.

The Company was advised on July 16, 1986 and December 16, 1986 that it is the subject of federal grand jury investigations in the Northern District of Illinois and the Western District of Washington, respectively. The Company believes that the investigations involve allocation of costs to government contracts. Under government procurement regulations, an indictment or conviction resulting from either investigation could result in the significant impairment or termination of Sundstrand Corporation's ability to receive new government contracts and the imposition of materially adverse fines and penalties.

Fourth quarter and total year 1986 results included a loss provision of $61.5 million before income taxes and $31.7 million after income taxes ($1.69 per share) for the ultimate resolution of government contract disputes in the Company's Aerospace business segment. Although the Company has not engaged in settlement discussions with the government, it is management's opinion that adequate provisions have been made for the resolution of government contract disputes, which may involve litigation and take an extended period of time.

Businesses Acquired and Sold

In July 1985, Sundstrand purchased the Turbomach Division of Solar Turbines Incorporated, a wholly owned subsidiary of Caterpillar Tractor Co. The cost of the acquisition was $102,000,000 of cash, a Sundstrand non-negotiable promissory note for $19,000,000 payable over seven years, and $2,300,000 of other acquisition costs. The acquisition has been accounted for as a purchase; the excess of cost over the net assets acquired was approximately $56,700,000 and is being amortized over 40 years.

In May 1984, Sundstrand acquired Wulfsberg Electronics, Inc. for 240,710 shares of Common Stock purchased on the open market for $10,657,000, net of $190,000 cash received from Wulfsberg. In November 1984, the Company acquired for $70,411,000, net of $3,340,000 cash received from Sullair, the remaining 89.5% outstanding shares of Sullair Corporation not previously owned by Sundstrand. Prior to 1984 Sundstrand had acquired 10.5% of Sullair stock for $5,872,000. The acquisitions of Wulfsberg and Sullair have been accounted for as purchases; the excess of cost over the net assets acquired was approximately $60,814,000 and is being amortized over 40 years.

Results of operations for Turbomach, Wulfsberg, and Sullair are included in the consolidated financial statements from dates of acquisition. The following table summarizes on an unaudited proforma basis, the combined results of operations as though Turbomach had been acquired on January 1, 1985.

	(Amounts in thousands except per share data)
	1985
Net sales	$1,324,538
Net earnings	73,923
Earnings per share	3.99

In November 1984, Sundstrand exchanged 154,057 shares of its Common Stock for all of the outstanding Common Stock of Signatron, Inc. The acquisition was accounted for as a pooling of interests.

Subsequent Event

On January 12, 1987, Sundstrand Corporation and Sauer Getriebe AG of Neumuenster, West Germany established a joint venture, combining their Hydraulic Power Systems businesses. Effective January 1, 1987, this new joint venture will have one operating group in the United States named Sundstrand-Sauer, and another in Europe named Sauer-Sundstrand. Klaus H. Murmann, a member of Sundstrand's Board of Directors, was the President and Chief Executive Officer of Sauer Getriebe AG. The joint venture management includes Mr. Murmann as a director and Chief Executive Officer, and Michael J. Draper from Sundstrand as a director and Chief Operating Officer.

Sales of Sundstrand's Hydraulic Power Systems business included in 1986 consolidated operating results were $119.4 million. Included in Sundstrand's consolidated balance sheet at December 31, 1986, were net assets of approximately $44.0 million, which have been contributed to the joint venture effective January 1, 1987. Future rental commitments under noncancelable operating leases beyond 1986 and building space for Sundstrand's Hydraulic Power Systems business were not included in the Supplementary Statement of Earnings Information footnote on page 34 and under Properties in the Additional 10K Information on page 41, respectively.

Sundstrand and Sauer are leading manufacturers of hydraulic power transmission equipment in both America and Europe, respectively. Each parent company holds a 50% interest in the joint venture, and it will be accounted for as an equity investment on the balance sheet of Sundstrand subsequent to December 31, 1986.

Quarterly Results (unaudited)

Selected unaudited quarterly financial data are shown below.

(Amounts in thousands except per share data)

Quarter	Net sales	Gross profit	Net earnings	Earnings	Dividends paid	Price range High	Low
1986							
First	$ 344,479	$113,831	$17,106	$ .92	$ .45	$64-3/8	$50-3/4
Second	343,291	120,402	19,739	1.05	.45	64-3/8	59-5/8
Third	348,505	120,982	20,083	1.07	.45	60-1/4	51
Fourth(a)	397,665	134,428	(11,528)	(.62)	.45	56-1/2	49-1/4
	$1,433,940	$489,643	$45,400	$2.42	$1.80		
1985							
First	$ 288,675	$ 99,009	$14,971	$ .81	$ .45	$49-1/2	$42-3/4
Second	303,667	104,481	17,528	.95	.45	46-1/4	40
Third(b)	317,411	110,509	19,053	1.03	.45	49-1/8	43
Fourth(b)	374,388	119,682	22,896	1.23	.45	54-3/4	42-3/4
	$1,284,141	$433,681	$74,448	$4.02	$1.80		

(Per share of Common Stock: Earnings, Dividends paid, Price range High/Low)

(a) Fourth quarter 1986 results include a loss provision for the ultimate resolution of government contract disputes. The effect of this loss provision was to reduce net earnings by $31.7 million ($1.69 per share).

(b) Effective January 1, 1985, Sundstrand changed its method of valuing certain subsidiaries' inventories to the LIFO method. The effect of this change was to reduce net earnings by $0.7 million ($.04 per share) and $1.1 million ($.06 per share) during the third and fourth quarters, respectively.

Auditor's Report

GrantThornton

Accountants and
Management Consultants

Member Firm
Grant Thornton International

Board of Directors and Stockholders
Sundstrand Corporation

We have examined the consolidated balance sheets of Sundstrand Corporation and Subsidiaries as of December 31, 1986 and 1985, and the related consolidated statements of earnings, changes in financial position, and stockholders' equity for each of the three years in the period ended December 31, 1986. Our examinations were made in accordance with generally accepted auditing standards, and accordingly included such tests of the accounting records and such other auditing procedures as we considered necessary in the circumstances.

In our opinion, the consolidated financial statements referred to above present fairly the consolidated financial position of Sundstrand Corporation and Subsidiaries at December 31, 1986 and 1985, and the consolidated results of their operations and changes in their financial position for the three years ended December 31, 1986, in conformity with generally accepted accounting principles applied on a consistent basis.

Chicago, Illinois
February 6, 1987

Grant Thornton

Management's Report

The management of Sundstrand is responsible for the preparation and presentation of the consolidated financial statements and related financial information included in this Annual Report. These have been prepared in conformity with generally accepted accounting principles consistently applied and as such include amounts based on estimates by management. The consolidated financial statements have been audited by the Company's independent accountants, Grant Thornton.

Management is also responsible for maintaining a system of internal accounting controls which is designed to provide reasonable assurance that assets are safeguarded and that transactions are executed in accordance with management's authorization and properly recorded. Judgments are required to assess and balance the relative cost and expected benefits of these controls. To assure the maintenance of effective internal controls, management adopts and disseminates policies, directives, and procedures, selects and trains qualified personnel, establishes an organizational structure which permits the delegation of authority and responsibility, and maintains an active program of internal audits and appropriate managerial follow-up.

The Board of Directors elects an Audit Committee from among its members, none of whom are employees of the Company. The Audit Committee meets periodically with management, the internal auditors, and the independent accountants to review the work of each and satisfy itself that they are properly discharging their responsibilities. Both the independent accountants and internal auditors have free access to the Audit Committee, without the presence of management, to discuss internal accounting controls, auditing, and financial reporting matters.

Ted Ross

Ted Ross
Vice President of Finance
and Secretary

Directors and Officers

Board of Directors

Evans W. Erikson
Chairman of the Board and Chief Executive Officer
Director 10 years

Don R. O'Hare
Vice Chairman of the Board
Director 8 years

David MacMorris
Executive Vice President
Sundstrand Corporation
Director 1 year

James Wm. Ethington[2,4]
Retired Chairman
Sundstrand Corporation
Director 28 years

Robert C. Hyndman[3]
Vice Chairman
Morton Thiokol, Inc.
Director 1 year

Thomas L. Martin, Jr.[1]
President
Illinois Institute of Technology
Chairman
Illinois Institute of Technology Research Institute
Director 8 years

Klaus H. Murmann[2]
Chief Executive Officer
Sundstrand-Sauer Company
Chairman of the Confederation
of German Industries
Director 6 years

Donald E. Nordlund[1]
Chairman and Chief Executive Officer
Staley Continental, Inc.
Director 11 years

Thomas G. Pownall[3,4]
Chairman and Chief Executive Officer
Martin Marietta Corporation
Director 9 years

John A. Puelicher[2,4]
Chairman of the Board and President
Marshall & Ilsley Corporation
Chairman of the Board
M&I Marshall & Ilsley Bank
Director 10 years

Ward Smith[1,3]
President and Chief Executive Officer
Nacco Industries, Inc.
Director 4 years

[1]*Nominating Committee*
[2]*Audit Committee*
[3]*Compensation Committee*
[4]*Finance Committee*

Officers

Evans W. Erikson
Chairman of the Board and Chief Executive Officer
Elected Chairman January 1, 1980. Age 60

Don R. O'Hare
Vice Chairman of the Board
Elected Vice Chairman January 1, 1980. Age 64

David MacMorris
Executive Vice President
Elected Executive Vice President February 21, 1985; for more than five years prior thereto Vice President and General Manager, Aviation Operations, of the Company's Advanced Technology Group. Age 63

Harry C. Stonecipher
Executive Vice President
Elected Executive Vice President December 1, 1986; Vice President and General Manager, Evendale Aircraft Engine Product Operations, General Electric Company from 1984 to December 1986 and Vice President and General Manager, Commercial and Military Transport Engine Operations, General Electric Company from 1982 to 1984. Age 50

Kenelm A. Groff
Vice President of Administration
Elected Vice President December 6, 1977. Age 57

A. Adrian Kemper
Controller
Elected Controller April 21, 1978. Age 54

Bernard W. Kittle
Group Vice President, Advanced Technology Group
Elected Vice President February 19, 1980. Age 55

William R. Kopp
Group Vice President, Data Control Group
Elected Vice President October 14, 1981. Age 49

Clark E. Lemke
Treasurer
Elected Treasurer December 8, 1983; Corporate Assistant Treasurer of Gould, Inc. from 1979 to 1983. Age 40

Philip W. Polgreen
Vice President, Personnel and Public Relations
Elected Vice President January 1, 1983; Vice President and Manager, Personnel Division of the Company from 1978 to 1982. Age 58

Ted Ross
Vice President of Finance and Secretary
Elected Vice President April 21, 1978. Age 55

Richard M. Schilling
Vice President and General Counsel
Elected Vice President April 21, 1978. Age 49

Review of Operations

	1986*	1985	1984
Summary of Operations			
Net sales			
Aerospace - Commercial	$ **377,628**	315,320	246,965
- Military	$ **590,412**	490,563	401,213
- Total Aerospace	$ **968,040**	805,883	648,178
Industrial	$ **465,900**	478,258	393,770
Total	$**1,433,940**	1,284,141	1,041,948
Operating profit			
Aerospace	$ **94,276**	131,631	98,740
Industrial	$ **6,346**	20,487	26,341
Total	$ **100,622**	152,118	125,081
Earnings before income taxes	$ **66,409**	119,692	111,650
Percent of net sales	**4.6%**	9.3%	10.7%
Net earnings	$ **45,400**	74,448	66,412
Percent of net sales	**3.2%**	5.8%	6.4%
Return on average total capital, after tax	**8.0%**	11.3%	11.2%
Return on average equity, after tax	**7.6%**	13.2%	12.8%
Per Share of Common Stock			
Earnings			
Primary	$ **2.42**	4.02	3.63
Fully diluted	$ **2.42**	4.02	3.63
Cash dividends	$ **1.80**	1.80	1.80
Market value - high	$ **64.38**	54.75	52.00
low	$ **49.25**	40.00	34.38
year-end	$ **53.25**	54.50	44.50
Stockholders' equity if dilutive securities converted	$ **32.24**	31.56	28.97
Year-End Financial Position			
Working capital	$ **414,207**	288,209	278,724
Current ratio	**2.6**	1.9	2.1
Total assets	$**1,399,176**	1,311,179	1,089,880
Long-term debt	$ **308,944**	238,063	174,352
Total debt	$ **317,165**	320,000	219,313
Stockholders' equity	$ **604,669**	589,129	535,785
Ratio of total debt to total capital	**34.4%**	35.2%	29.0%
Other Data			
Orders received			
Aerospace	$ **974,850**	988,252	712,000
Industrial	$ **471,301**	479,065	397,034
Total	$**1,446,151**	1,467,317	1,109,034
Unfilled orders			
Aerospace	$ **952,880**	946,010	763,641
Industrial	$ **113,275**	107,874	107,067
Total	$**1,066,155**	1,053,884	870,708
Property, plant, and equipment (excludes leased equip.):			
Additions, at cost	$ **111,539**	109,382	93,205
Depreciation	$ **70,670**	59,811	51,754
Approximate number of employees	**16,000**	16,100	15,200
Approximate number of stockholders of record	**5,900**	6,900	7,500

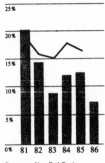

Return on Year-End Equity
percent

▬▬▬ Fortune 500 Top Quartile

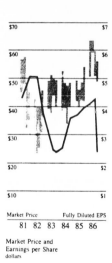

Market Price	Fully Diluted EPS
81 82 83 84 85 86	

Market Price and
Earnings per Share
dollars

Price
(Quarterly ranges)

Fully Diluted EPS
(12 months ended)

(Dollar amounts in thousands except per share data)

					Year ended December 31,		
1983	1982	1981	1980	1979	1978	1977	1976
226,252	276,829	294,857	307,572	203,832	141,906	139,888	121,809
340,765	283,231	229,452	171,804	147,267	124,405	118,610	114,460
567,017	560,060	524,309	479,376	351,099	266,311	258,498	236,269
342,301	401,513	521,378	446,650	491,531	465,264	402,701	366,331
909,318	961,573	1,045,687	926,026	842,630	731,575	661,199	602,600
84,581	87,421	89,238	85,333	52,702	39,710	29,665	30,954
7,478	25,787	95,721	76,345	71,517	56,585	48,381	44,492
92,059	113,208	184,959	161,678	124,219	96,295	78,046	75,446
70,563	105,351	156,541	121,857	100,175	75,844	58,389	53,204
7.8%	11.0%	15.0%	13.2%	11.9%	10.4%	8.8%	8.8%
44,240	69,300	95,011	76,907	66,274	49,052	36,861	33,745
4.9%	7.2%	9.1%	8.3%	7.9%	6.7%	5.6%	5.6%
8.5%	12.4%	17.9%	16.2%	15.5%	13.0%	11.3%	10.7%
8.9%	14.5%	22.1%	21.0%	21.4%	18.7%	16.7%	18.1%
2.42	3.77	5.23	4.45	3.98	3.00	2.32	2.18
2.42	3.77	5.15	4.21	3.67	2.72	2.10	1.96
1.80	1.80	1.70	1.50	1.05	.73	.60	.48
51.75	46.00	58.25	59.50	40.00	28.00	21.38	18.56
37.88	23.25	32.75	34.75	21.75	15.81	16.00	8.50
48.75	44.00	42.00	56.50	38.00	22.00	18.00	17.81
27.35	26.72	25.17	21.56	18.92	16.31	14.55	13.16
306,207	303,233	349,246	344,701	265,038	226,844	208,780	184,885
2.7	2.5	2.6	3.1	2.4	2.4	2.6	2.6
916,712	895,314	892,894	786,694	706,303	623,854	569,611	513,183
131,530	135,825	150,496	179,086	149,342	155,773	176,915	181,171
154,318	175,663	182,235	185,242	187,621	185,286	183,789	189,947
500,399	489,001	465,412	396,204	336,085	283,721	239,877	200,616
23.6%	26.4%	28.1%	31.9%	35.8%	39.5%	43.4%	48.6%
601,399	570,856	564,840	617,135	562,878	337,947	297,015	224,447
351,536	335,272	514,772	432,637	478,512	484,332	400,160	335,938
952,935	906,128	1,079,612	1,049,772	1,041,390	822,279	697,175	560,385
699,819	665,437	654,641	614,110	476,351	264,572	192,936	154,416
103,803	94,568	160,809	167,415	181,428	194,447	175,379	177,923
803,622	760,005	815,450	781,525	657,779	459,019	368,315	332,339
81,752	70,262	64,726	64,713	44,462	44,189	42,880	41,745
46,687	41,714	36,256	30.483	29,535	31,554	26,217	23,129
13,400	13,100	16,100	15,600	15,400	15,700	14,300	14,500
7,400	8,300	9,400	8,900	8,600	8,900	9,000	9,100

*1986 includes a loss provision of $61.5 million before income taxes and $31.7 million after income taxes ($1.69 per share) for the ultimate resolution of government contract disputes in the Company's Aerospace business segment.

Additional 10K Information

Date of Incorporation. Sundstrand was incorporated in Illinois in 1910 and became a Delaware corporation in 1966.

Materials and Supplies. Sundstrand utilizes many raw materials of primary and alloy type metal in forms such as cast, forged, sheet, and bar, which are available from numerous sources. Sundstrand also utilizes structural parts composed of fiber reinforced plastic materials which are obtained from various sources. In addition, mechanical and electronic components such as fasteners, bearings, gaskets, filters, motors, resistors, transformers, and semiconductors are procured from various sources. Sundstrand deals with over 2,000 suppliers and is not dependent upon any one manufacturer of parts or supplier of raw materials or services. However, from time to time general shortages of particular raw materials and components may have an adverse effect on the Company.

Patents. Sundstrand owns a large number of patents (expiring between 1987 and 2004) which are of importance in the aggregate to the conduct of its business and are expected to be of value in the future. In the judgment of the Company, its patents are adequate for the conduct of its business, but the loss or expiration of any single patent or group of patents would not materially affect the conduct of its business as a whole. In the Company's opinion, its design, manufacturing and marketing skills, experience, and reputation are more responsible for its positions in the industries it serves than its patents.

Properties. Sundstrand occupies building space totalling approximately 6,992,000 square feet and is divided by business segment as follows: Industrial, 3,246,000 square feet; Aerospace, 3,633,000 square feet; and Corporate offices, 113,000 square feet. All plants are owned by the Company except approximately 878,000 square feet of leased space, and are well maintained, in good operating condition, and suitable for its operations. The Company owns approximately 202 acres of vacant land for future expansion.

Domestic manufacturing facilities are located in Rockford, Illinois; Michigan City, Indiana; Lexington, Massachusetts; Camdenton, Missouri; Dowagiac, Michigan; Denver, Arvada, and Grand Junction, Colorado; York, Nebraska; Redmond and Moses Lake, Washington; San Diego, Costa Mesa, Irvine, Brea, and Newbury Park, California; Prescott and Phoenix, Arizona; Milwaukee, Wisconsin; and Auburn, Alabama. Foreign manufacturing facilities are located in the Republic of Singapore; Dijon, France; Rexdale, Ontario, Canada; and Sao Paulo, Brazil.

Sundstrand also leases to the Sundstrand-Sauer joint venture manufacturing facilities located in LaSalle and Freeport, Illinois; and Ames, Iowa. The space in these facilities totals approximately 829,000 square feet.

Competition. Sundstrand has competitors or potential competitors in each of its product lines. Some of these competitors or potential competitors may have greater financial and personnel resources than the Company. Sundstrand believes that research and development has been of particular significance to the Company's competitive standing in each segment of its business.

Legal Proceedings. During 1983, a complaint was filed in the Circuit Court for Cass County, Michigan by the Attorney General for the State of Michigan against Sundstrand Heat Transfer, Inc., Dowagiac, Michigan, a subsidiary of Sundstrand. The complaint seeks injunctive relief, penalties, and damages. Sundstrand Heat Transfer, Inc. has taken action to eliminate sources of trichloroethylene (TCE) contamination and has installed and is operating equipment which is removing the TCE from its surface water discharge and from the groundwater, thereby meeting all requirements of the preliminary injunction which was issued in 1984. The complaint is still pending before the Cass County Circuit Court.

Sundstrand has been notified by the United States Environmental Protection Agency ("USEPA") that it and others are potentially responsible parties under the Comprehensive Environmental Response, Compensation and Liability Act of 1980 ("Superfund") with respect to a number of sites at which environmental damage is alleged. A variety of relief, including remedial action, is sought in connection with these sites. In those instances where the Company has determined it to be appropriate, it has joined with other potentially responsible parties and entered into consent orders with the USEPA, and if applicable, state environmental agencies, providing for the performance of certain remedial action and site investigation to determine what, if any, additional remedial actions should be taken.

The Company believes that it will not incur a material liability or expenditure in connection with these matters.

Supplemental Stockholder Information

Annual Meeting

The Company's Annual Meeting will be held in the Renaissance Suite, Salon A, The Helmsley Palace, 455 Madison Avenue, New York, New York, on Thursday, April 16, 1987 at 10:30 o'clock in the morning, Eastern Time.

Form 10K

A copy of the Company's Annual Report to the Securities and Exchange Commission on Form 10K is available on written request. However, all information required under Parts I, II, and III of Form 10K has been incorporated by reference to the Annual Report to Shareholders or the proxy statement.

Common Stock (SNS) Information

Transfer Agent, Registrar, and Dividend Disbursing Agent:
The First National Bank of Chicago
One First National Plaza
Chicago, Illinois 60670
Listing:
Midwest Stock Exchange
New York Stock Exchange
Pacific Stock Exchange

Dividend Reinvestment Plan

Sundstrand offers to its common stockholders a dividend reinvestment program. The Plan provides a simple, cost-free way of automatically putting stockholder dividends to work as well as making voluntary cash investments. The Company absorbs brokerage commissions and bank service fees for all participants.

Written Request Information

Information about Form 10K and the Dividend Reinvestment Plan is available upon written request to:
Stockholder Relations
Sundstrand Corporation
4751 Harrison Avenue
P.O. Box 7003
Rockford, Illinois 61125-7003

SNS is the symbol for Sundstrand
Corporation on the New York, Midwest,
and Pacific Stock exchanges.

INDEX

About the Author

JOHN P. FERTAKIS is Professor of Accounting and Business Law at Washington State University. A certified Cost Analyst, he has written widely for publications such as *The Journal of Accounting Research, The Accounting Review, Management Services, The Journal of Accountancy*, and *Management Accounting*.